THE
KITCHEN PANTRY
SCIENTIST

CHEMISTRY FOR KIDS

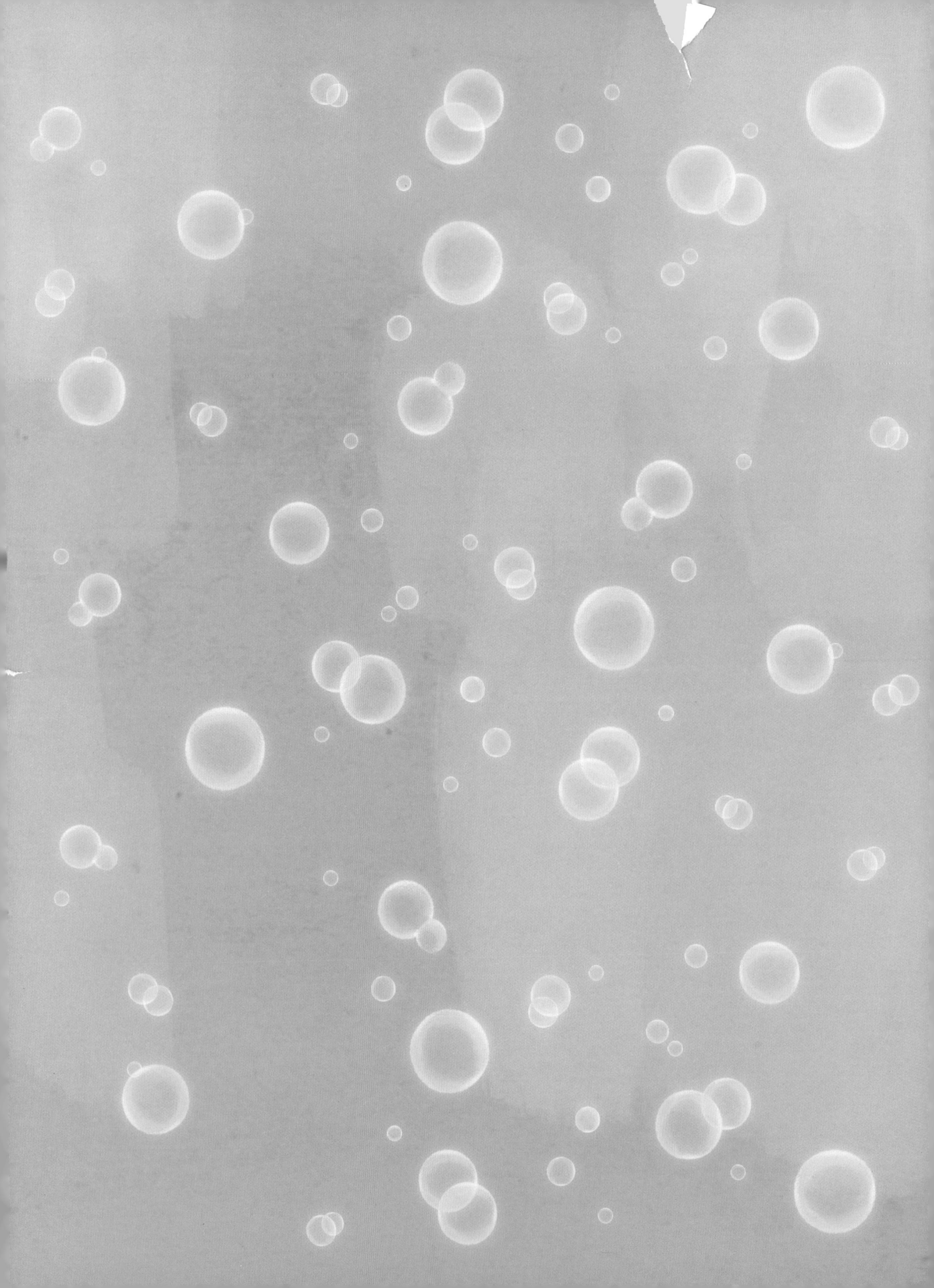

THE
KITCHEN PANTRY
SCIENTIST

CHEMISTRY FOR KIDS

Homemade Science Experiments and Activities Inspired by Awesome Chemists, Past and Present

LIZ LEE HEINECKE

Brimming with creative inspiration, how-to projects, and useful information to enrich your everyday life, Quarto Knows is a favorite destination for those pursuing their interests and passions. Visit our site and dig deeper with our books into your area of interest: Quarto Creates, Quarto Cooks, Quarto Homes, Quarto Lives, Quarto Drives, Quarto Explores, Quarto Gifts, or Quarto Kids.

First Published in 2020 by Quarry Books, an imprint of The Quarto Group,
100 Cummings Center, Suite 265-D, Beverly, MA 01915, USA.
T (978) 282-9590 F (978) 283-2742 QuartoKnows.com

10 9 8 7 6 5 4 3

ISBN: 978-1-63159-830-2

Digital edition published in 2020
eISBN: 978-1-63159-831-9

Library of Congress Cataloging-in-Publication Data

Names: Heinecke, Liz Lee, author.
Title: The kitchen pantry scientist: chemistry for kids: homemade science
experiments and activities inspired by awesome chemists, past and
present / Liz Heinecke.
Description: Beverly, MA : Quarry Books, an imprint of The Quarto Group,
2020. | Series: The kitchen pantry scientist's guides | Includes index.
| Audience: Ages 7-12.
Identifiers: LCCN 2019050167 (print) | LCCN 2019050168 (ebook) | ISBN
9781631598302 | ISBN 9781631598319 (ebook)
Subjects: LCSH: Chemists--Biography--Juvenile literature. |
Chemistry--Experiments--Juvenile literature. |
Chemistry--History--Juvenile literature.
Classification: LCC QD21 .H45 2020 (print) | LCC QD21 (ebook) | DDC
540.92/2--dc23
LC record available at https://lccn.loc.gov/2019050167
LC ebook record available at https://lccn.loc.gov/2019050168

Design: Debbie Berne
Cover Illustrations: Kelly Anne Dalton; Mattie Wells
(Author illustration, also on page 3)
Photography: Amber Procaccini Photography
Illustrations: Kelly Anne Dalton

Printed in China

CONTENTS

*approximate date

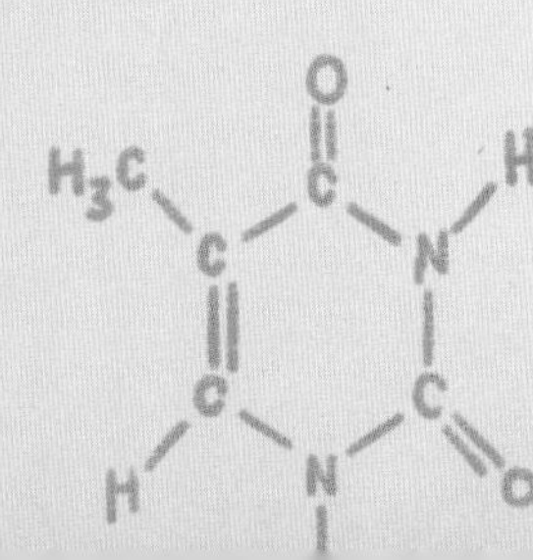

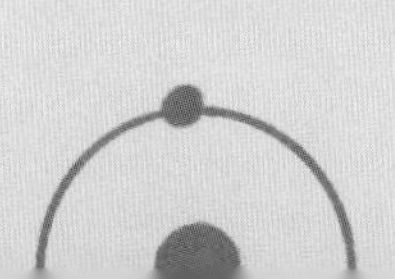

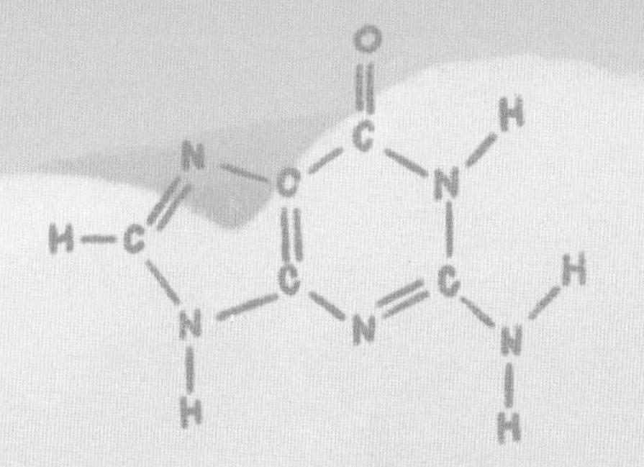

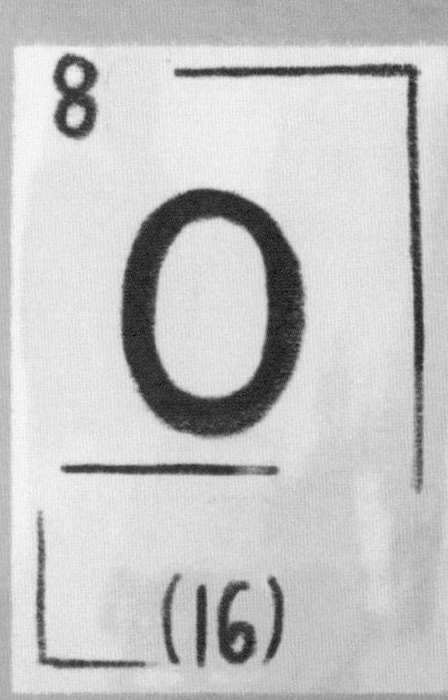
8
O
(16)

84
Po
(209)

88
Ra
(226)

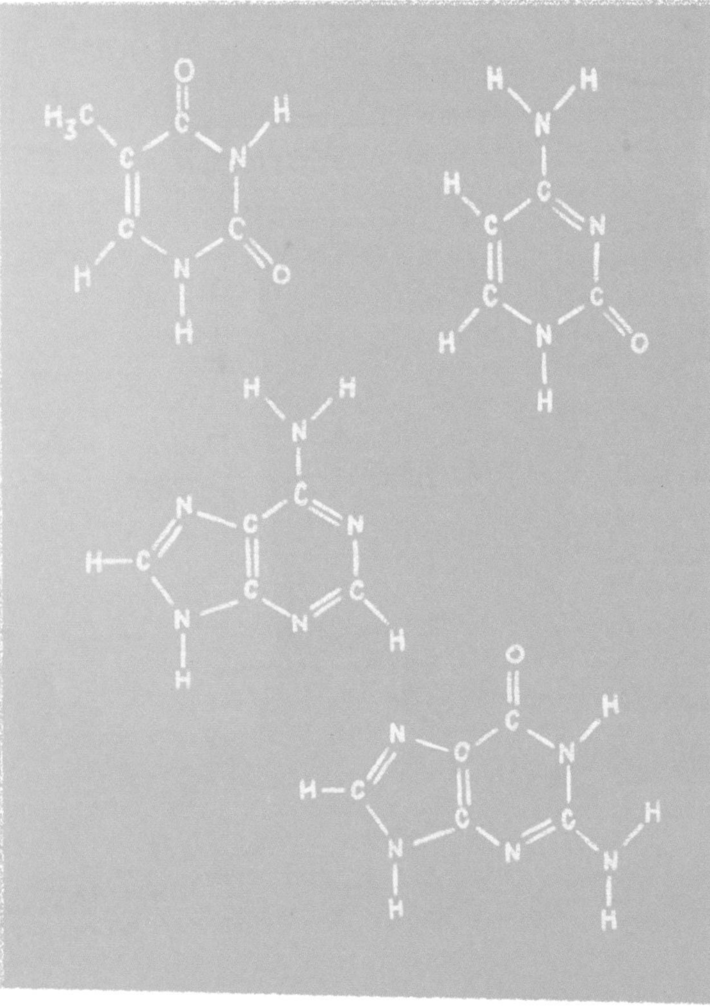

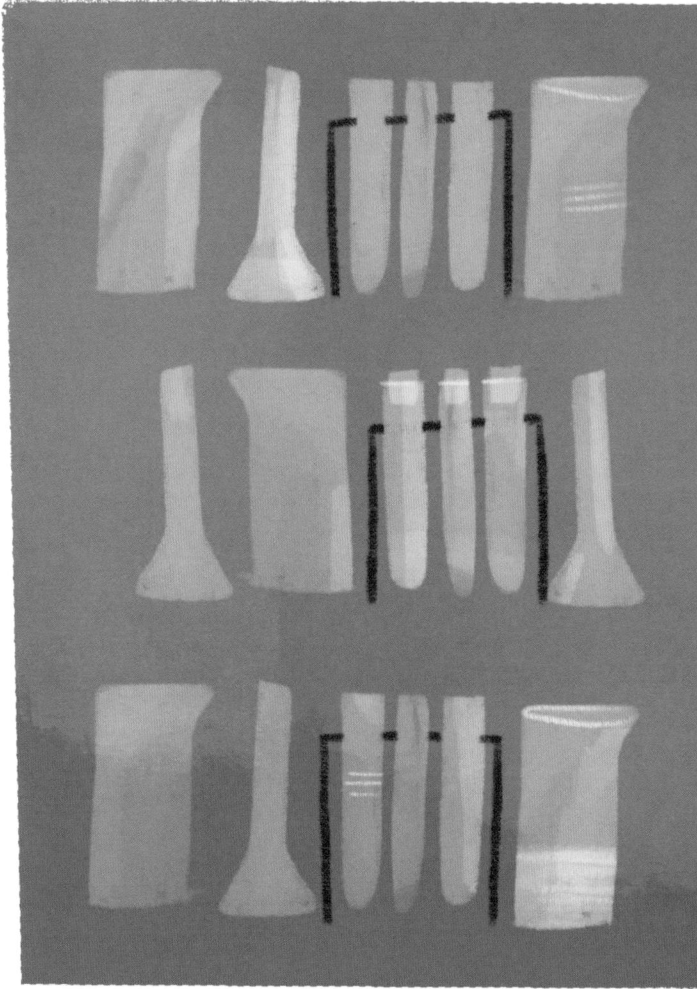

INTRODUCTION

People have been tinkering with chemistry for thousands of years. We have always loved to play with fire, stirring things together, and boiling crazy concoctions. It's fun to imagine what interesting, beautiful, and useful chemical mixtures were created back when *Homo sapiens* (humans) first arrived on the scene.

We know that early humans ground up natural pigments such as ochre and used them to tint animal blood, creating durable paint that we can still see on cave walls today. Archeologists speculate that certain ancient mixtures may have been used for protection against sun and insects or for preserving animal hides. It's funny to think that even cave people needed bug spray.

Over the next 70,000 years or so, as civilizations took hold around the globe, a large portion of humanity found themselves settling down. After countless generations of life on the road, they now had crops, animals, and villages to protect. People still didn't have a word for chemistry, but they learned to make better medicines and discovered how to extract and mix metals that could be molded into cooking vessels, weapons, and jewelry. Early chemists such as Tapputi-Belatikallim and Galen fermented wine, distilled perfume and alcohol, made soap, and perfected natural inks and dyes. Eventually the invention of gunpowder changed the course of history forever.

Modern chemistry was born around 250 years ago, when measurement, mathematics, and the scientific method were officially applied to experiments that lots of people were doing in laboratories and kitchen sinks. In 1869 after the first draft of the periodic table was published by a man named Mendeleev, scientists rushed to fill in the blanks.

The elemental discoveries that followed gave scientists, for the first time in history, the tools to visualize atoms, the building blocks of matter. They worked to understand this fascinating new phenomenon and soon had a model for it that featured negatively charged particles called electrons whizzing, like Saturn's rings, around a dense nucleus. Since then, discovery has accelerated at breakneck speed. At times, the products of modern chemistry have caused heartbreaking, unthinkable harm, but more often than not, chemistry makes our lives better.

The Kitchen Pantry Scientist: Chemistry for Kids is a series of snapshots of twenty-five chemists, from ancient history through today. Each lab tells the story of a phenomenal scientist, along with some background about their work and where you can still find it used or reflected in today's world. A step-by-step illustrated experiment is paired with each story to offer readers a chance to get their hands on the concepts pursued by each scientist. Readers can distill perfume using a method created in ancient Mesopotamia by a woman named Tapputi-Belatikallim or replicate a chemical reaction similar to one Marie Curie used to purify radioactive elements. Curious minds will discover an inspiring group of role models and many memorable experiments in the pages of this book.

LAB 1

Tapputi-Belatikallim b. 1200 BCE*

FRAGRANCE DISTILLATION

ROYAL PERFUMER

Over 3200 years ago in ancient Mesopotamia, a pen made from a reed inscribed the name Tapputi-Belatikallim in a soft clay tablet. Today the cuneiform notches and figures remain, and scholars who can read the ancient script tell us that she held an important post as the manager of the royal household. Thanks to the scratches in baked clay, which held its form as the centuries rolled by, we understand that Tapputi, whose second name means "overseer," prepared fragrances for the king and his family. The royals used some of the scents she prepared as perfume and saved others to offer to the gods during religious rituals.

MESOPOTAMIA

Ancient Mesopotamia lay between two rivers, the Tigris and the Euphrates, in a land known as the Fertile Crescent where Iraq and parts of Iran, Syria, and Turkey are found today. The fertile land gave birth to the first known cities: agriculture arose on the land, people began to domesticate animals, and written language developed. Mesopotamia was a center for culture and language and gave rise to the wheel, the chariot, and the writings of a high priestess named Enheduanna, the world's first author known by name.

TRANSCENDENT SCENTS

When Tapputi made her mark as the world's first recorded chemist around 1200 BCE, tendrils of fragrance were intertwined in social order, religion, and medicine. Tapputi and her contemporaries believed that the invisible, beautiful scents they offered could transcend the physical world to reach their gods, who would be pleased by their sacrifice. Kings were self-proclaimed conduits to the gods, anointed with the most valuable perfumes, while fragrant ointments and salves were used by healers as well.

ROYAL RECIPE

Tapputi's recipe for a perfume included preparing a mixture of oil, flowers, and a lemon-grass-type herb called calamus and then steeping the mixture with other fragrant substances before filtering and distilling it again and again. The distillates and oils she created served as salves and perfumes for the king. Her complicated, multi-step extraction method was recorded around 1200 BCE. An ancient copy of her recipe includes the first description of a distillation apparatus ever recorded and a number of her methods are still used today in modern perfume production.

MODERN FRAGRANCE

Chemical engineers today use several of the same techniques that Tapputi used, but on a much larger scale, to create today's fragrances.

* approximate date

FRAGRANCE DISTILLATION

Distill essential oils from citrus, flowers, and herbs using expression and distillation methods similar to those used by Tapputi-Belatikallim over 3000 years ago.

Fig. 4. Wrap plant material in cheesecloth and place in steaming basket.

MATERIALS

- Slow cooker or pot with a domed lid and heatproof handle
- Steaming basket or small colander
- Small, heatproof bowl
- Fresh or dried lemon, herbs, or flowers
- Cheesecloth
- Rolling pin, mallet, or meat-tenderizing tool
- Small bottle and eyedropper (optional)
- Water

SAFETY TIPS AND HINTS

- Adult supervision is required for use of the stove or slow cooker.
- Lemon peel, rosemary, peppermint, and lavender work very nicely for this experiment. Fresh flowers work as well. You'll need large numbers of blossoms.

PROTOCOL

1 Add a few inches (5 cm) of water to the bottom of the slow cooker. Position a steaming basket or colander inside. The water level must be below the bottom of the steamer so that the flowers or herbs will sit above it in the water. Use jar lids to raise the basket if needed.

2 Place a small bowl at the center of the basket. Place the lid upside down on the pot to make sure it fits tightly. You may need to invert the steaming basket. Remove the lid.

3 If you are extracting essential oils from flowers, remove the petals from the stems, and discard the stems and leaves. *Fig. 1.*

4 For citrus scent, zest a lemon. For herbs, remove the leaves from the stems and discard the stems. *Fig. 2.*

5 Place the flower petals, lemon zest, or herbs on a large piece of cheese-cloth. Crush them with a rolling pin, mallet, or meat-tenderizing tool. *Fig. 3.*

6 Fold the cheesecloth over to envelop the plant material, roll the plant material in the cheesecloth. Place the cheesecloth in the steaming basket and put the steaming basket in the pot. *Fig. 4.*

7 Position a small bowl on the cheese-cloth so that the inverted lid handle will drip into it, and put the lid on the pot tightly. *Fig. 5.*

8 Heat the pot using the lowest heat possible. Place ice in the center of the upside-down lid to speed up condensation.

9 Check the pot frequently to see how much liquid has collected in the small bowl. When the desired amount has accumulated, turn off the slow cooker or stove. Allow everything to cool.

10 Smell your creation. Were you able to capture the scent? Pour the distilled liquid into a small jar or vial. Label it. *Fig. 6.*

11 Mix with other essential oils you make to create a unique fragrance.

Fig. 1. Remove blossoms or leaves from stems.

Fig. 2. Grate citrus peels.

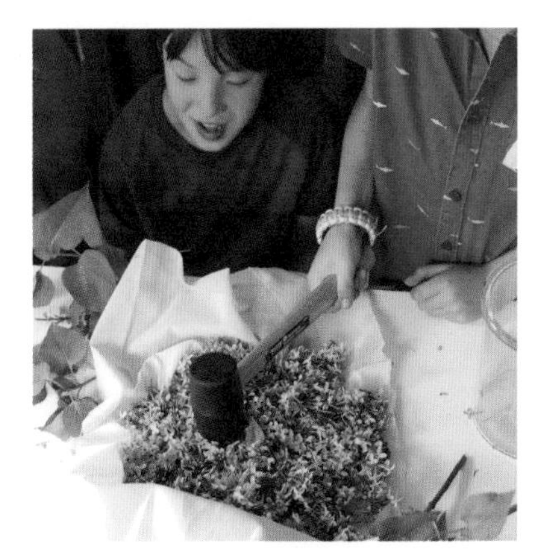
Fig. 3. Crush fresh blossoms and herbs.

Fig. 5. Position steamer in a pot containing a few inches (5 cm) of water. Invert lid over collection bowl.

Fig. 6. Add essential oils to labeled storage containers.

CREATIVE ENRICHMENT

Add crushed flowers to warm oil. Let the mixture sit, and then filter out the plant fragments with a sieve or cheesecloth to trap essential fragrance in the oil. Compare the scent of flowers captured by oil to the smell of essential oils distilled using the technique in this lab.

THE STORY BEHIND THE CHEMISTRY

ESSENTIAL OILS

Expression is a scent-extraction method. It involves pressing plant cells to squeeze out the fragrant oil. In this lab, flowers, citrus peels, or herbs are crushed to break the plant cells open and free up scent-laden molecules, commonly called essential oils. These compounds are volatile, which means that they will quickly evaporate into the air when heated up. Certain essential oils can be destroyed by overheating, so they must be heated very slowly to release the best-smelling product. Depending on the desired scent, multiple steps and techniques may be required to achieve the perfect fragrance.

DISTILLATION

The technique of distillation allows crushed flowers or plants to be gently heated over water, so that steam moves through the material, carrying the essential oils to a cooled surface where the purified liquid condenses into droplets and is collected. The scented distillate can then be mixed with other fragrances, added to alcohol to make a fast-drying perfume, or mixed with oils and other substances to create balms and lotions.

SIMPLE SCENTS

In this lab, flowers, citrus peels, or herbs are crushed and added to a homemade distillation apparatus to collect scented distillate that can be combined with other scents to create unique fragrances.

LAB 2

Galen b. 129 CE*

SOAP

DOCTOR TO GLADIATORS AND PLAGUE VICTIMS

The Roman physician known today as Galen went by many names, including Galen of Pergamon, the city in present-day Turkey where he was born around 129 CE. His father was a wealthy architect who exposed Galen to politics, philosophy, and the books in the city's world-famous library. Legend has it that Galen's father had a dream that his son should be a physician, so Galen began to study medicine and to treat Romans visiting Pergamon's temple in search of medical assistance.

GLADIATOR DOCTOR

When Galen was nineteen, his father died and left him wealthy. Galen continued his medical studies, traveling to Crete, Cyprus, and the great medical school of Alexandria. At the age of twenty-eight, he became a physician to the gladiators of the High Priest of Asia and ran a trauma center where he learned to mend broken bones. He began to view open wounds as "windows into the body" that left patients vulnerable to infection, and observed a link between hygiene, nutrition, and health. During the time he acted as the gladiators' doctor, surprisingly few of his patients died from their injuries.

A PLAGUE

Galen eventually became a physician to Roman emperors and began to write extensively about medicine. During his tenure as royal physician, a disease called the Antonine Plague struck Rome. Historians believe that it was probably smallpox and may have killed over half of the Roman Empire's population. Galen was interested in diagnosing and treating the disease, offering patients a prognosis (prediction) of what would happen based on what he'd learned from his research. He was also a philosopher and believed that there was an inseparable link between the mind and the physical body.

AN AUTHOR

Galen wrote an enormous body of literature on medicine and philosophy, summarizing the work of physicians who came before him such as Hippocrates and adding what he'd learned, making Greek medicine world famous. His writings include references to soap, saying that it acts as a medicine acting to remove impurities from the body and from clothing. Historians believe that this may be the first reference in literature to soap being used as a detergent. With his interest in hygiene, it's not surprising that Galen wrote about soap, singling out a high-fat German concoction as his favorite. Today soap-making is an enormous industry, and consumers have hundreds of sudsy bars and liquids to choose from.

* approximate date

SOAP

The Greek physician Galen understood that good hygiene was essential to good health. He wrote about soap in his books, recognizing the importance of this chemical concoction used to clean skin and clothes. In this lab, you'll melt glycerin to mold your own bars of soap.

MATERIALS

- "Melt and pour" soap base (see Resources Page 121)
- Microwave or stove
- Glass jars and bowls
- Craft sticks for stirring (optional)
- Essential oils (optional)
- Skin-safe soap colorants (optional)
- Dried flowers, herbs, oatmeal, or citrus peels (optional)
- Small plastic figures (optional)
- Soap molds or silicone molds
- Rubbing alcohol in a spray bottle (optional)

SAFETY TIPS AND HINTS

- If you use rubbing alcohol (isopropanol) to remove bubbles, work in a well-ventilated area and supervise young children.
- Food coloring generally doesn't work well for coloring soap and will stain skin.
- Wear safety glasses when spraying alcohol.

Fig. 6. It's fun to embed plastic figures in clear soap.

PROTOCOL

1 Get your soap-making supplies ready, including materials for coloring, decorating, and scenting your cosmetic creations (if using). ***Fig. 1.***

2 Add a few small pieces of soap base to a microwavable container and melt for 30 seconds at a time, stirring in between, until the soap is liquid.

3 Pour the melted soap base into a jar or bowl. Add coloring and fragrance, if desired. Mix in seeds, oatmeal, or other small items you want suspended in the soap. ***Fig. 2.***

4 Pour the soap mix into a mold and tap it to remove bubbles. Rubbing alcohol may be sprayed on the soap's surface to pop tiny bubbles. ***Fig. 3.***

5 Soap may be added in layers for interesting effects or be painted onto the mold to make stripes before more soap is added. ***Fig. 4.***

6 Get creative with shape, color, and texture. ***Fig. 5.***

7 It's fun to embed plastic figures like animals in the soap. Homemade soap makes a great gift. ***Fig. 6.***

Fig. 1. Gather supplies for making soap

Fig. 2. Add color and texture to soap.

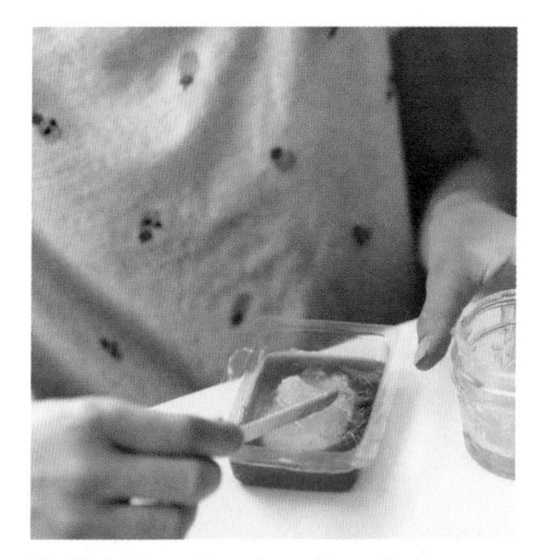

Fig. 3. Add soap base to molds and remove bubbles.

Fig. 4. Soap base can be added in layers.

Fig. 5. Get creative!

CREATIVE ENRICHMENT

Make your own essential oil to add fragrance to you soap. (Lab 14)

THE STORY BEHIND THE CHEMISTRY

Fats called triglycerides are used to make soap, and they also make up most of the fats and oils we eat. Composed of alcohols and fatty acids, they are the building blocks of both plant and animal fats, including olive oil, coconut oil, butter, and bacon fat.

Soap is made using a process called saponification, which involves mixing animal or vegetable fats with a strong base, which is a chemical that has a high pH (Lab 12). The chemical reaction between the fatty acids and the base separates fatty acid salts (soap) from a compound called glycerol. Whether the resulting soap is liquid or solid depends on the type of base used.

Making soap the "old-fashioned way" is time-consuming and somewhat hazardous. It requires combining fat with lye, which scientists call sodium hydroxide. To make lye, ashes from a hardwood fire are boiled in rainwater. The solids are allowed to sink to the bottom and the lye, which can burn skin and clothing, is skimmed off the top. Lye is combined with fat or oil and left to cure for several weeks until the entire substance has transformed into soap.

LAB 3

Jabir ibn Hayyan b. 815 CE*

EVAPORATION

PRACTICAL ALCHEMIST

Jabir ibn Hayyan, whose name appears on a number of ancient manuscripts related to chemistry, medicine, and alchemy, is often referred to as the "Father of Chemistry." An early science explorer by that name authored one or more important books, but science historians today believe that his followers and a number of other brilliant individuals probably contributed to the large body of work that has been attached to his name.

THE PHILOSOPHER'S STONE

Historians believe that Jabir, who later became internationally known as Geber, lived and worked in modern-day Iran or Iraq. Writings attributed to him include subjects such as mathematics, physics, chemistry, and medicine. In Jabir's time, alchemy was all the rage. Scholars believed that all matter was composed of fire, water, earth, and air and that by using a mythical substance known as "the philosopher's stone," one substance could be rearranged into another.

EVAPORATION

Evaporation occurs when the liquid in a substance vaporizes into a gas, leaving most of the solids in the solution behind. For example, ocean water constantly evaporates into the air, but the salt stays in the sea. Heat speeds up the evaporation of water, so by heating a solution over a fire, early scientists like Jabir ibn Hayyan were able to use evaporation equipment to quickly vaporize liquids.

FIRE AND WATER

In his quest to find the philosopher's stone and understand the nature of matter, Jabir created a number of techniques to analyze earth and rocks. Fire and water were readily available tools, and he made good use of them. Jabir is credited with having improved existing distillation and evaporation equipment and inventing several other types of scientific apparatus as well.

PRACTICAL SCIENCE

Crystallization, distillation, isolation of acids, and the purification of the elements sulfur, mercury, and arsenic are all attributed to Jabir ibn Hayyan. Like chemists today, he and his followers also used chemistry to invent method for practical applications. He is said to have created a substances that could be used to inhibit rust, and make cloth waterproof. Legend has it that he even invented a luminescent (glow-in-the-dark) ink.

* approximate date

EVAPORATION

A chemist called Jabir ibn Hayyan, or Gerber, described some of the earliest recorded studies on the science of evaporation and distillation. Create beautiful evaporation rings and learn why scientists today are still interested in how liquids dry.

Fig. 6. Take a digital image of the rings to magnify them.

MATERIALS

- White vinegar
- Small cups or bowls
- Liquid food coloring
- Measuring cups and spoons
- Cornstarch
- Small, flat, white plates or shallow white bowls (heatproof, not plastic)
- Baking sheet
- Stopwatch or timer
- Oven mitt
- Magnifying glass or digital camera, such as a phone camera

SAFETY TIPS AND HINTS

Adult supervision is recommended. Open the oven door to let vinegar fumes escape before removing hot plates and dishes from the oven.

PROTOCOL

1 Preheat the oven to 200°F (93°C). Measure ¼ cup (60 ml) of vinegar into each of three cups. *Fig. 1.*

2 Choose two colors to mix, such as blue and green or red and yellow. Add 5 drops of one color and 5 drops of the second color to each cup and mix well. *Fig. 2.*

3 Add ½ teaspoon of cornstarch to one of the cups of vinegar and food coloring. Mix it in and label the container. To a different cup, add a tiny pinch of cornstarch. Label and mix well. *Fig. 3.*

4 Use a spoon to measure enough vinegar and food coloring solution onto one of the small plates to generously cover the bottom of the plate. Count and record the number of spoonfuls you add and add an equal amount of the other two solutions to two more plates so that each plate is covered with one of the solutions. *Fig. 4.*

5 Place the plates on a baking sheet and put the baking sheet in the preheated oven. Set a stopwatch to record evaporation time, and check the plates every 10 minutes or so.

6 When the last drop of liquid has evaporated from each of the plates, remove the plates and record the time on the stopwatch. Evaporate the vinegar in the oven. Compare evaporation patterns. *Fig. 5.*

7 Write down your observations about the evaporation patterns on each plate. Use a digital device to photograph the rings and zoom in to magnify the edges. Note any color separation and record whether the ring boundaries are smooth, jagged, or fractal-like patterns. *Fig. 6.*

8 Repeat the experiment using different colors. How does drying the plates at room temperature affect evaporation? *Fig. 7.*

Fig. 1. Measure vinegar.

Fig. 2. Add food coloring.

Fig. 3. Add cornstarch to two of the containers

Fig. 4. Transfer solution to plates.

Fig. 5. Dry and compare the evaporation patterns on the plates.

Fig. 7. Repeat the experiment using different colors and different temperatures.

CREATIVE ENRICHMENT

Add different substances such as crushed chalk or flour to the vinegar-food coloring mix to see how they affect evaporation. Try using water as a base, rather than vinegar to see how evaporations time and patterns are affected.

THE STORY BEHIND THE CHEMISTRY

If you've ever seen the dried-out pattern left by spilled coffee, you know that after the water has evaporated, the majority of the leftover brown particles form a ring around the edges. Scientists who study this phenomena have discovered that particles in a droplet organize themselves in ringlets as the liquid dries.

The liquid in a droplet or on a plate is shaped like a shallow dome that is thick in the middle and unimaginably thin around the edges. Molecules in an evaporating solution don't stay still. Physical forces keep them moving and drive them toward the edge of the droplet and only the smallest particles in a solution find space at edges of the liquid. They remain there as the water molecules escape into the atmosphere.

Vinegar evaporates faster than water and adding heat speeds up the evaporation process. The smallest particles ring the very edges of the evaporation pattern while larger particles, like cornstarch, are stuck in the middle.

Scientists have discovered that by drying droplets, they can separate some of the proteins suspended inside of a single drop of human cells. Researchers hope that this work will help them create inexpensive disease-diagnosis kits.

8
O
(16)

LAB 4

Joseph Priestley b. 1733

CARBONATION

ISOLATOR OF OXYGEN AND CREATOR OF CARBONATION

Joseph Priestley was a minister, a teacher, a writer, a philosopher, and a politician with an enviable group of acquaintances, including Antoine Lavoisier (Lab 5). He is most famous for isolating oxygen and for inventing carbonation. Like his friend Benjamin Franklin, he dabbled in experimenting with electricity as well.

A CURIOUS MIND

From a young age, Joseph Priestley observed the world around him with curiosity. Born in England in 1733, he was bounced from house to house after his mother died and his father remarried. Eventually he ended up living with a wealthy aunt and uncle who recognized his intellectual brilliance. As a boy, Joseph recalled catching spiders in jars and wondering why they died when the lid was tightly shut. Later in life, those childhood experiments would influence his greatest discovery when he studied the gases in air.

A CHAMPION OF EDUCATION

After studying the ancient languages, math, and natural philosophy, which would soon be known as the natural sciences, Joseph got a job as a minister in a church. His ideas were too controversial for his congregation, so he went to work as a teacher instead. He wrote a textbook on grammar and in 1862 he married a woman named Mary Wilkinson. Priestley wrote history books around that time as well and made progressive arguments that universities should teach modern languages and practical skills. He also believed that educating women was important.

KITCHEN SINK SCIENTIST

When he decided to write a book on the history of electricity, Joseph Priestley met Benjamin Franklin and other luminaries in that field who encouraged him to try the experiments he was writing about for himself. Priestley's book became the new standard textbook about electricity, and included some of his original experiments and observations. Between 1774 and 1786, Joseph wrote a six-volume book about his experiments on air. He was the first scientist to isolate oxygen, although he clung to an old, incorrect theory about combustion (burning). This led him to argue with Antoine Lavoisier, who was doing precise measurements in his "new chemistry" and had a better understanding of the science of oxygen.

POP SCIENCE

In 1767 Priestley invented artificially carbonated water by hanging a filled vessel of water over a fermentation vat at a beer brewery to see whether the gas would deposit bubbles in the water. When the experiment worked, he took it to his lab, where he used a chemical reaction between an acid and a base to add bubbles to a drink that became known as "soda water." He called it his "happiest discovery." Today, beverage factories force carbon dioxide into cold water under high pressure to make soda.

CARBONATION

Joseph Priestley carbonated water using chalk and sulfuric acid. In this lab, you'll carbonate water using carbon dioxide gas you create by mixing baking soda and vinegar.

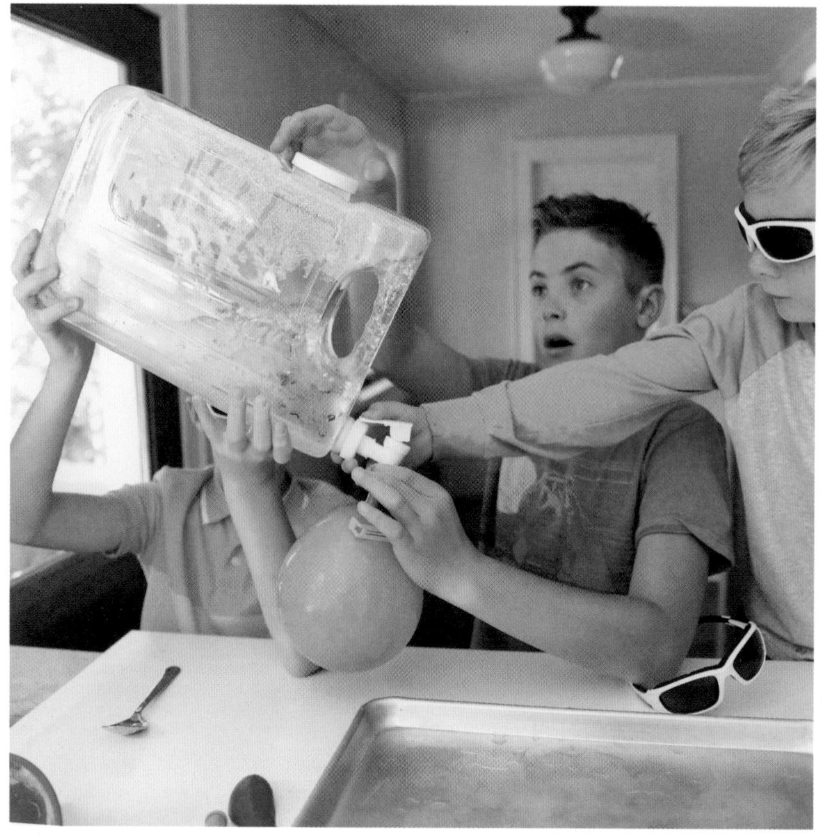

Fig. 6. Bubble the carbon dioxide gas through the water.

MATERIALS

- Empty 16- or 20-oz (474 to 591 ml) bottle
- Baking sheet
- White vinegar
- Baking soda
- Balloons
- Water dispenser with a spigot and a lid that can be tightened (see Resources page 121)
- Clamp, such as a chip-bag clamp or twist tie
- Funnel (optional, but helpful)
- Sugar cubes (optional)

SAFETY TIPS AND HINTS

- You need more than one person to do this project!
- Wear safety glasses or sunglasses while inflating balloons in case they burst.

PROTOCOL

1 Fill the water dispenser with a spigot about halfway full with ice-cold water.

2 Set an empty bottle on a baking sheet. Add vinegar to the bottle and fill to within a few inches (5 cm) of the top.

3 Use a funnel or a spoon to add 2 teaspoons (9 g) of baking soda to a balloon. ***Fig. 1.***

4 Put the mouth of the balloon over the mouth of the bottle so that no air can leak out. Pinch it between your thumb and finger to hold it on when you inflate the balloon. ***Fig. 2.***

5 Start the chemical reaction by shaking the baking soda from the balloon into the vinegar in the bottle. Carbon dioxide gas will start to form and inflate the balloon immediately. ***Fig. 3.***

6 When the balloon is fully inflated, pull it off the bottle and clamp it shut to trap the carbon dioxide gas inside. Remove it from the bottle before it gets so full that it pops. ***Fig. 4*** and ***Fig. 5.***

7 Carefully put the mouth of the balloon over the spigot. Unscrew the container's lid so that extra air can escape. Remove the clamp from the balloon and open the spigot so that the carbon dioxide gas in the balloon can bubble up through the water. ***Fig. 6.***

8 Immediately tighten the lid on the container to trap the carbon dioxide inside. ***Fig. 7.***

Fig. 1. Add baking soda to a balloon

Fig. 2. Put the balloon on the bottle and hold it in place.

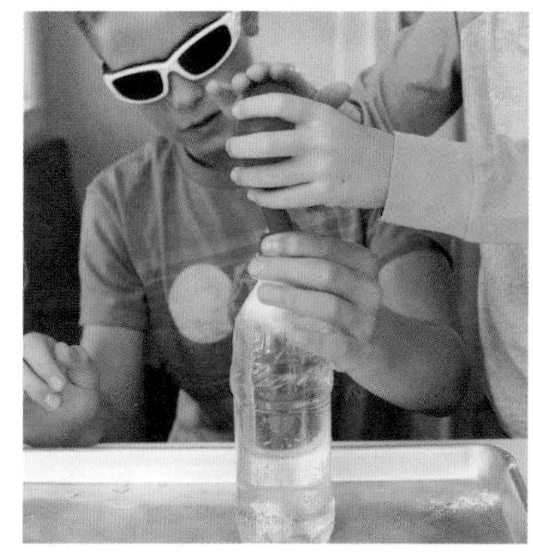

Fig. 3. Shake the baking soda into the balloon to start the chemical reaction.

Fig. 4. Pull the filled balloon off of the bottle and clamp it.

Fig. 5. Carbon dioxide gas will be trapped inside the balloon.

Fig. 7. Tighten the lid on the container to trap the carbon dioxide gas.

9 Rock the container gently back and forth to incorporate the carbon dioxide gas into the water. ***Fig. 8.***

10 Repeat steps 2 through 9 three or four times, so that you bubble several balloons full of carbon dioxide gas through the cold water in the spigot container. Taste the soda water. If it's not fizzy enough, let it sit in the refrigerator for a while and rock it again. Then add more carbon dioxide. ***Fig. 9.***

Optional: You can also carbonate lemonade using the chemical reaction between baking soda and the citric acid in lemons. Simply shake some sugar cubes in baking soda in a bag. ***Fig. 10.***

11 Drop the baking soda–coated sugar cubes in lemonade. ***Fig. 11.***

12 The chemical reaction makes carbon dioxide bubbles. Taste your delicious carbonated beverage. ***Fig. 12.***

Fig. 8. Rock the container to incorporate the gas.

Fig. 9. Taste the "soda water."

Fig. 10. Shake sugar cubes with baking soda.

Fig. 11. Drop the baking soda–coated sugar cubes in some lemonade

THE STORY BEHIND THE CHEMISTRY

Chemical reactions occur when two or more materials called reactants are mixed together to create some new chemical compounds, called products. While Joseph Priestley mixed sulfuric acid with powdered chalk (calcium carbonate) to carbonate water, this lab accomplishes the same task with safer ingredients. Whether you mix sulfuric acid and chalk or baking soda and vinegar, you synthesize one of the same products: carbon dioxide gas, which is more commonly called CO_2.

Carbon dioxide can be dissolved in water, but water molecules are only mildly attracted to CO_2. Dissolved carbon dioxide exists as individual CO_2 molecules surrounded by water molecules, rather than as bubbles. Under cold conditions in a closed container, carbon dioxide and water molecules are held together by their fleeting attraction and the gas remains dissolves into the water.

As carbonated water warms, the carbon dioxide molecules break free, gather in bunches, and float to the surface as bubbles. Bubbles in carbonated beverages also like to form on tiny imperfections on surfaces, such as ice cubes, glasses, bottles, and even Mentos mints. That's why soda foams when you pour it over ice.

Fig. 12. Taste the carbonated lemonade!

CREATIVE ENRICHMENT

Try this experiment using red cabbage juice (Lab 15) to see how carbon dioxide reacts with water to make it more acidic. As the water absorbs the carbon dioxide gas, you will see the color turn from purple or blue to pink or red.

LAB 5

Antoine Lavoisier b. 1743

OXIDATION

FIRST MODERN CHEMIST

Antoine-Laurent Lavoisier made the jump from qualitative chemistry, which is descriptive, to quantitative chemistry, which depends on measurement. Besides making a number of important discoveries in chemistry, he saw scientific discovery as a way to improve people's lives. Tragically his involvement in local government and industry proved fatal in the end, when he was beheaded during the French Revolution.

SHARING HIS WEALTH

Antoine's mother died when he was only five years old, and he inherited a large fortune. Born to a wealthy Parisian family in 1743, he was educated in the best schools and studied a number of disciplines in college, including math, botany, geology, and astronomy. Lavoisier also earned a law degree, which he never used because he was passionate about science and wealthy enough to pursue it without an income. Believing that public science education was essential to society, he built a laboratory where his less-wealthy colleagues could experiment, and he was involved in the creation of two organizations that worked to educate the public about science.

A PARTNER IN SCIENCE

When he was twenty-eight years old, Antoine Lavoisier married Marie-Anne Pierrette Paulze, who became interested in chemistry, and was trained in science by two of Lavoisier's colleagues. The famous painter Jacques-Louis David, who would later paint a famous portrait of the Lavoisiers, taught her to make accurate drawings and soon Marie-Anne accompanied Lavoisier to the laboratory each day as his laboratory assistant. In the lab, she took measurements, kept detailed notes, and sketched their experiments. An accomplished illustrator, Marie-Anne also served as his translator because he only spoke French and many important scientific papers of the time, such as those of Joseph Priestley (Lab 5), had been published in English.

QUANTITATIVE CHEMISTRY

Out of all of his extraordinary discoveries, the most groundbreaking thing that Lavoisier did was to measure and record the results of his experiments. Lavoisier designed scales that could measure tiny changes in weight very accurately, and he discovered that in an ordinary chemical reaction, the weight or mass of the substances that reacted was equal to the total weight of the products of the chemical reaction. This allowed him to discover the law of the "conservation of mass" by repeating the experiment over and over, taking precise measurements each time. In 1789 Lavoisier published the first-ever textbook of chemistry based on quantitative experiments.

DISSECTING AIR

Lavoisier experimented extensively with combustion, or burning, which produces chemicals containing oxygen, although at the time, no one knew what oxygen was. Antoine observed that when he burned different substances, although the total weight of ashes and air didn't change, the ashes were heavier than the starting material, which suggested that they'd combined with something from the air. He also observed that burning different substances produced "air" with different qualities, including breathability and flammability.

A SAD ENDING

Antoine Lavoisier received many awards during his lifetime, but he was beheaded in 1794, during the Reign of Terror in the French Revolution when he was only fifty years old. His laboratory equipment has been preserved for the public in Musée des Arts et Métiers in Paris. Since Lavoisier's time, quantitative measurement has played an essential role in scientific experimentation.

OXIDATION

Create an oxidation reaction using steel wool and vinegar. Measure the temperature change created by the chemical reaction.

MATERIALS

- 2 pads of steel wool (see Resources page 121)
- White vinegar
- 1 or 2 digital thermometers
- 2 clear containers with lids (A plate will work as a cover.)

PROTOCOL

1 Rinse soap out of pretreated steel wool. Cover one steel wool pad with vinegar.

2 Make sure that the vinegar is soaked through. *Fig. 2.*

3 Squeeze extra vinegar from the steel wool, dump out the vinegar, and return the wet steel wool to the container. *Fig. 3.*

4 Record the starting temperature on a thermometer. Next, wrap the vinegar-soaked steel wool around the thermometer and secure it with a rubber band. *Fig. 4.*

5 Cover the container with a lid. Watch the thermometer to see what happens to the temperature. Record the temperature every 30 seconds until the temperature stops climbing. *Fig. 5.*

Fig. 6. Cover the container and observe the temperature change.

6 The temperature rises as the steel wool oxidizes. You may see moisture condense on the inside of the covered container. *Fig. 6.*

7 After a few hours, reddish rust will be visible on the steel wool. Allow it to dry and continue to rust. In a few days, it will disintegrate into red dust if you put it in a plastic bag and crush it with your fingers. *Fig. 7.*

CREATIVE ENRICHMENT

Make your own wood stain from rust and vinegar, by soaking steel wool in vinegar in an open container for three days. Filter the mixture with cheesecloth, saving the rust-stained vinegar. Let it sit for another day or two and brush it on to different types of wood to see how well it stains.

Fig. 1. Immerse one steel wool pad in vinegar.

Fig. 2. Make sure that the vinegar is soaked through.

Fig. 3. Wring out the steel wool

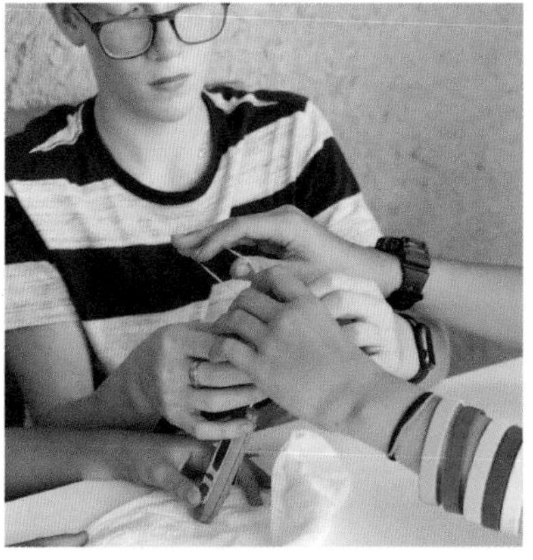

Fig. 4. Wrap the vinegar-soaked steel wool around a thermometer and secure.

Fig. 5. You may see condensation on the container.

Fig. 7. Rust will form on the steel wool.

THE STORY BEHIND THE CHEMISTRY

Steel is made of iron combined with a small amount of dissolved carbon. The combination is extremely strong and cheap to produce, and steel can be found in many things you encounter every day, from buildings to appliances to automobiles. Steel wool is made up of fine filaments that have been coated with oil, so that the iron in them won't react with the oxygen and moisture in the air and start to rust. Steel wool pads for cleaning also may contain soap, which should be rinsed out to perform this lab.

Chemical reactions called oxidation reactions occur when the atoms in a substance give away negatively charged electrons. The electron-donating substance is said to be oxidized. Vinegar, which is an acid, strips the protective coating off of the steel wool, exposing it to the water in the vinegar, which is made up of hydrogen and oxygen. Iron and oxygen react and combine as electrons move from the oxygen atoms to the iron, forming compounds that look red or brown. This process is called rusting and it occurs more quickly in an acidic environment.

Oxidation is an exothermic chemical reaction, which means that it gives off heat. In this lab, you can see that the temperature of the vinegar-soaked steel wool is higher than the temperature of untreated steel wool. This measurable difference indicates that the iron in the pad is undergoing oxidation and is rusting. As the steel wool continues to rust, the red-brown iron oxides will become visible. Rusting and combustion, or burning, are both oxidation reactions.

LAB 6

Alessandro Volta b. 1745

CHEMICAL BATTERIES

INVENTOR OF THE BATTERY

Alessandro Volta was a physicist who loved reading about all kinds of science and was ecspecially interested in the work being done on flammable gases. Although his main focus was electricity, he used chemistry in his research every day and his keen awareness of natural philosophy, including the study of animals, aided in him in the invention of the battery.

POPULAR SCIENCE

Alessandro Volta was born in Como, Italy, in 1745. Like most scientists of the time, he had been born into a wealthy family. His parents wanted him to study law, but he was hooked on electricity by the time he was a teenager and abandoned school to pursue his experiments. At the time, the study of electricity was fairly new, and people experimented with it in their parlors to create shocking demonstrations.

AN ELECTRIC TEACHER

When he wasn't teaching grammar, Volta played with electrical charge in the laboratory of a friend. By 1775, he'd invented an apparatus that he called an electrophorus that could carry charge from one object to another. Intrigued by Benjamin Franklin's research on flammable gas, he was the first scientist to isolate methane, which he discovered bubbling up in a swamp near his home. Alessandro then proceeded to experiment with igniting the gas using an electrical spark.

FROG LEGS

One of Volta's colleagues had discovered that it was possible to make frog legs hanging on a brass hook jump by touching them with a different type of metal and believed that the frog legs were the source of some sort of "animal electricity." Volta disagreed believing that the two different metals must be creating the electrical charge and that the frog's legs simply carried the charge. He proved this by replacing the frog legs with a salt water–soaked cloth, which also conducted a current.

ELECTRIC STINGRAY

Based on his results, Volta made a stack of more than thirty alternating zinc and silver disks separated by pieces of salt water–soaked cloth. It was fashioned after the stinging organ of an electrical stingray, which was also called a torpedo fish. When he connected the two ends of the stack to a metal wire, current flowed through the wire. Alessandro Volta had invented the first battery, which he called an "artificial electric organ." Today chemical batteries are used to power up everything from game controllers to cars.

CHEMICAL BATTERIES

Alessandro Volta stacked metal disks to make his battery. While he used salt water as his conducting material, this lab uses the acidic juice inside lemons as the electrolyte, which carries the electrical current.

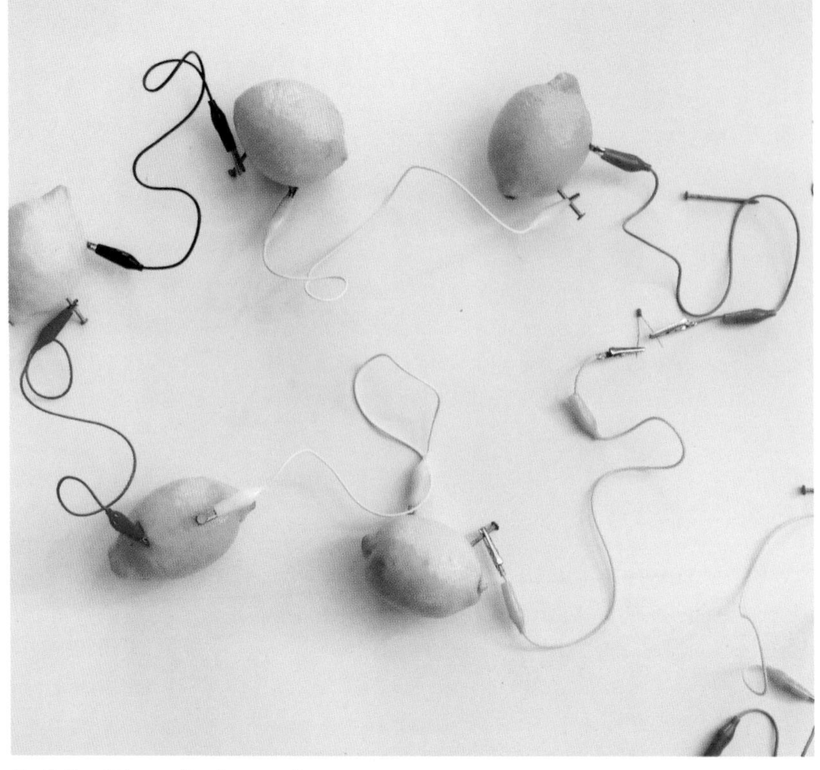

Fig. 7. Try adding another lemon or two.

MATERIALS

- 6 very juicy fresh lemons
- 6 copper pennies or 6 short pieces of copper wire
- White vinegar for cleaning pennies (optional)
- 6 zinc-coated (galvanized) nails, around 2 inches (5 cm) long
- 7 test leads with alligator clips on each end
- 5mm LEDs (light-emitting diodes) (see Resources page 121)
- Ruler
- Voltmeter (optional)

SAFETY TIPS AND HINTS

- Adult supervision required if using a sharp knife, but a butter knife will work for cutting slits in lemons.
- This experiment can be tricky. The lemons have to be juicy enough or it may not work. Try adding more lemons to the battery if your LED doesn't light up. The light may be very faint.

PROTOCOL

1 Roll 4 lemons on a hard surface to release the juice inside. ***Fig. 1.***

2 If using pennies as your copper electrode, first soak them in vinegar, and wipe them off to clean them. Use a knife to make a penny-sized slit in each lemon. ***Fig. 2.***

3 Insert zinc nails about 1 inch (3 cm) from the cuts you made for the pennies. ***Fig. 3.***

4 Position pennies in the slots so that they stick up out of the lemons. If using copper wire instead of pennies, insert it about 1 inch (3 cm) away from the zinc nails. ***Fig. 4.***

5 Connect the alligator clips from lemon to lemon, from penny to nail, penny to nail, and so on, so that the lemons are connected in a semicircle with a loose lead on either end. One loose lead should be connected to copper, and the other one to a zinc nail. ***Fig. 5.***

6 Connect an LED to the two free alligator clips. If it doesn't light, try connecting the clips to the opposite legs of the LED. If you have a voltmeter, use it to test how much power you're generating. ***Fig. 6.***

7 If the LED won't light up, try adding another lemon to the battery. ***Fig. 7.***

CREATIVE ENRICHMENT

Try this experiment using potatoes or pickles. Use a voltmeter to compare your batteries.

Fig. 1. Roll lemons to release the juice.

Fig. 2. Make slits for the pennies.

Fig. 3. Insert the zinc nails.

Fig. 4. Position pennies or wire about 1 inch (3 cm) from the zinc nails.

Fig. 5. Connect the lemons from penny to nail with the alligator clips.

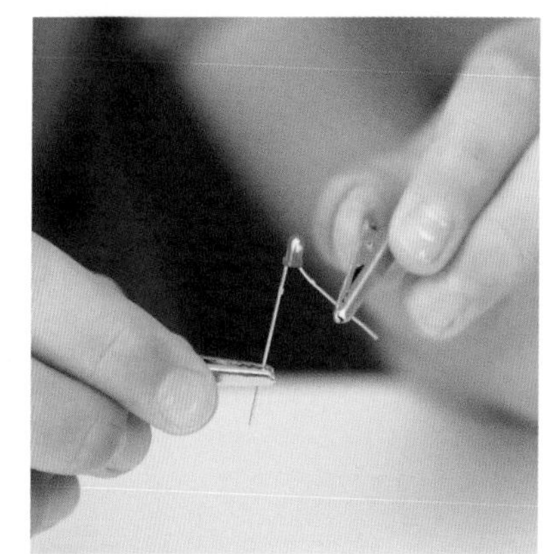

Fig. 6. Connect an LED.

THE STORY BEHIND THE CHEMISTRY

Batteries are devices that contain chemical energy with the potential to be converted into electrical energy. Lemon, zinc, and copper are not batteries on their own, but the moment you poke a zinc nail and a penny into a lemon, you trigger chemical reactions that free up the electrical potential of the combined objects.

There are three parts to a battery: a negatively charged cathode, a positively charged anode, and an electrolyte. In the case of our lemon battery, the zinc nail plays the role of anode, copper is the cathode, and acidic lemon juice acts as the electrolyte, which is a fluid containing electrically charged particles. Make sure you know which is the anode and which is the cathode. A chemical reaction between the lemon juice and the zinc nail causes negatively charged electrons to build up on the zinc. If given a connection to the copper, these excess electrons will happily race through a metal wire from zinc to copper.

When you put a zinc nail in a lemon, some of the zinc starts to dissolve in the acidic lemon juice. There is chemical reaction between the zinc and the lemon juice called an oxidation reaction, which releases negatively charged particles called electrons. Copper reacts with the citric acid differently than zinc does and electrons start to flow through the wire from the zinc nails to the copper. The more lemons you hook to a battery, the more zinc is dissolving, the more electrons are flowing, and the more power you can generate.

LAB 7

William Henry Perkin b. 1838

SYNTHETIC DYES

COLLEGE AT FIFTEEN

William Henry Perkin was born in London in 1838. The youngest of seven children, he demonstrated a talent for science from a young age and entered the Royal College of Chemistry when he was only fifteen years old. Soon he began working with a professor named August Wilhelm von Hoffman.

COAL TAR

In the nineteenth century, candles had been mostly replaced by gas lights and the industrial waste left behind from coal gas production was a dark, noxious liquid called coal tar. Based on his knowledge of chemistry, Professor Hoffman hypothesized that a malaria medicine called quinine could be synthesized from certain components of coal tar called amines. He assigned Perkin to this project and the young chemist was so excited about it that he started to work on it while he was home on vacation,

KITCHEN SINK SCIENCE

Experimenting in a homemade lab on the top floor of his parent's house, Perkin's first attempt at making quinine from a coal tar amine called toluene failed, so he tried again, using a different amine called benzene. Adding sulfuric acid and potassium dichromate to benzene produced a sticky black substance, rather than the clear quinine he was attempting to produce.

AN UNEXPECTED RESULT

When Perkin went to clean the glassware from the failed experiment, it was stained purple. Rinsing the beaker with alcohol to remove the purple transferred the brilliant color to the cleaning cloth he was using, staining it a lovely color, which was not easily washed out. Perkin, who had unsuccessfully tried to synthesize synthetic dye in the past, was astonished and had the vision to realize that the unexpected results of his experiment had the potential to make him very wealthy. He set up a workspace in a garden shed and along with his brother and a friend, tested the dye and scaled up its production.

PATENT SUCCESS

When he was only eighteen years old, William Perkin filed for and was awarded a patent on his discovery. The dye, which he named Tyrian purple, was soon nicknamed "mauve" after a purple flower, and later called mauveine by chemists. It was a smashing success. Mauve-dyed textiles were rich in color, but not prohibitively expensive to produce. Soon people everywhere, from Queen Victoria to working-class women, were wearing the trendy color. Perkin's dye, along with his creation of a mordant, or fixative, for synthetic dyes, revolutionized the fashion industry.

SYNTHETIC DYES

Use food coloring or drink concentrates to dye yarn or create colorful hair streaks. These brilliant chemical compounds are related to purple aniline dye, which was first concocted in 1856 by William Henry Perkin.

Fig. 8. Rinse yarn with water and air dry.

MATERIALS

- White- or cream-colored wool yarn
- White vinegar
- Small bowls or jars
- Liquid food coloring or drops of colorful drink mix, such as Kool Aid
- Scissors

SAFETY TIPS AND HINTS

- Wear old clothes. Food coloring stains clothing and skin.
- Use yarn with the highest wool content available. Synthetic yarn may not work.
- For dark hair, a concentrated paste made from drink mix and water may work better.

PROTOCOL

1 Wind the yarn around your fingers to create a small bunch. Tie it together. *Fig. 1.*

2 Add enough vinegar to a small bowl to cover the yarn. Soak the yarn in vinegar for 10 to 15 minutes. *Fig. 2.*

3 Add ½ cup (120 ml) of vinegar to several small bowls or jars, depending on how many colors you want to use. To this, add several drops of food coloring or drink mix to each container until you see a rich, dark color. Mix well. *Fig. 3.*

4 Add the yarn to the food coloring and vinegar mixture. *Fig. 4*

5 Soak yarn in the dye for 15 minutes to 1 hour. *Fig. 5.*

6 Alternately separate some strands of hair to dye and soak them in vinegar for 5 minutes and then in vinegar tinted with several drops of food coloring for 15 minutes to 1 hour. *Fig. 6.*

7 Rinse the yarn with water and air dry. Find a creative use for your beautifully dyed project. *Fig. 7.*

8 If you dyed your hair, rinse it well with water and dry it to avoid transferring color to your clothing. *Fig. 8.*

CREATIVE ENRICHMENT

Soak hard-boiled eggs in vinegar and dye them using the same technique.

Fig. 1. Wind yarn and tie.

Fig. 2. Presoak wool yarn in vinegar.

Fig. 3. Add food coloring or drink mix to vinegar.

Fig. 4. Add yarn to food coloring–vinegar mixture.

Fig. 5. Soak yarn in dye.

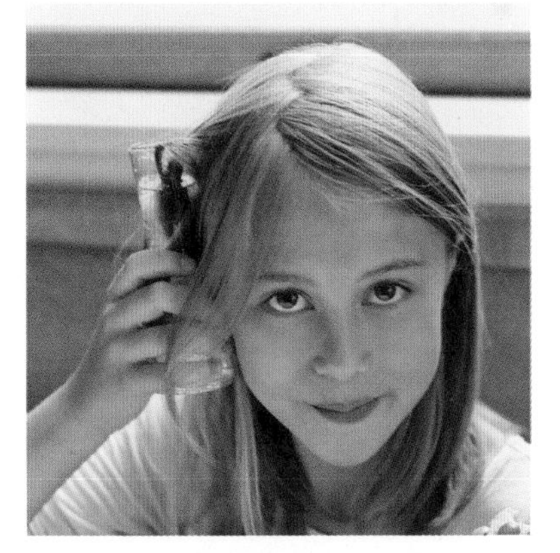

Fig. 6. Alternately soak hair in vinegar and then food-coloring vinegar.

THE STORY BEHIND THE CHEMISTRY

Until William Henry Perkin figured out how to synthesize his mauve dye from coal tar, purple textile dye was incredibly difficult and expensive to produce. Historically purple had been considered a "royal" color, because only the very wealthy could afford it and the best dye, Tyrian purple, could be extracted only from the secretions of a certain species of sea snail.

NO MORE SNAILS

Following Perkin's discovery, a rainbow of new synthetic dye colors was extracted from coal tar, including magenta, red, pink, and indigo. They are usually large, stable molecules that contain ring structures made of carbon and hydrogen, and their color depends on how the chemicals absorb light.

VINEGAR BATH

Acid dyes, such as food coloring, work best in an acidic environment. Vinegar is acetic acid diluted with water and is perfect for dying wool. Under acidic conditions, natural fibers (wool and hair) attract the dye like magnets, allowing hydrogen bonds to form between the fibers and the colorful molecules.

IN TODAY'S WORLD

Today anilines are mostly used for the production of plastics and polymers, they're also used to make acetaminophen and the indigo dye in the blue jeans you wear.

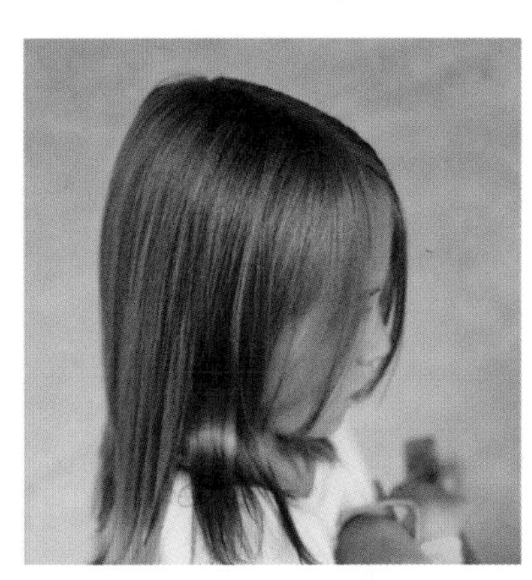

Fig. 7. Rinse hair with water and dry.

0
I
II
III
IV
V
VI
VII
VIII

LAB 8

Dmitri Mendeleev b. 1834

THE PERIODIC TABLE

A DIFFICULT CHILDHOOD

Life was not easy for Dmitri Mendeleev and his family, but his mother recognized his genius early on and made it possible for him to reach his full potential. Born in Siberia in 1834, Dmitri was the youngest of twelve children. The year he was born, his father went blind and his mother went to work full-time to run her family's glass factory to support their children. When Dmitri was thirteen, his father died. Soon afterwards the factory burned down and his mother took him to St. Petersburg so that he could receive an education. Not long after arriving in St. Petersburg, Dmitri's mother died too.

AN EDUCATION

At sixteen years old, Mendeleev entered college to become a teacher, like his father had been. He loved chemistry and by the time he was twenty, he was publishing research papers. Much of his research was done in a laboratory he'd set up in his apartment, Dmitri struggled with bouts of an infectious disease called tuberculosis throughout his life. After moving a few times, he returned to St. Petersburg to finish his graduate degree and teach at the university.

A REVELATION

Unable to find an inorganic chemistry textbook that he considered good enough for his students, Mendeleev decided to write one himself. He'd already written a book on organic chemistry in the space of a few months. As he wrote, he compared the properties of all of the chemical elements known at the time, and he noticed similarities between elements with similar atomic weights. He tried different ways of organizing the elements based on their groups and atomic weights. Legend has it that he fell asleep at his desk and worked the elemental puzzle out in a dream. When he awoke, he organized the same periodic table we use today, minus the elements that had yet to be discovered.

MORE THAN A TABLE

In addition to organizing the table, Mendeleev was able to predict elements that had not yet been isolated that would one day fill the gaps in his table. He made a number of additional contributions to science in the fields of hydrodynamics, meteorology, and petroleum chemistry, among others. As women entered the university in Russia for the first time, Dmitri Mendeleev volunteered to teach them, without pay. Scientists and students around the world still use the periodic table every day.

THE PERIODIC TABLE

Dmitri Mendeleev noticed that elements with similar atomic weights had other similarities and used this observation to assemble the periodic table of the elements. In this lab, you'll assemble your own periodic table to see how he helped to organize inorganic chemistry.

Fig. 3. Label the containers

MATERIALS

- 118 small, clear containers with lids, such as disposable sample cups or clear plastic ornaments
- Periodic table of elements (see page 122-123)
- Large piece of cardboard or wood to organize the containers onto
- Permanent marker
- Small objects to represent protons and neutrons (see safety tips below.)
- Glue or a hot glue gun

SAFETY TIPS AND HINTS

Choose tiny objects like paper punch circles or cake sprinkles to represent protons and neutrons. Write "10" on some of the punched circles to represent 10 protons or neutrons or use large sprinkles to represent 10 protons and neutrons and smaller sprinkles to represent single protons and neutrons. Adult supervision is recommended when using a glue gun.

PROTOCOL

1 Study the periodic table on pages 122-123. Organize the clear containers by looking at the periodic table so that you have one container to represent each element. *Fig. 1.*

2 Find the atomic number from the atomic mass. Add sprinkles or other small objects to represent protons and neutrons. To figure out how many neutrons there are, subtract the atomic number from the atomic mass. *Fig. 2.*

3 Label each container with the name of the element it represents. *Fig. 3.*

4 Keep in mind that you'll have to fit more than 200 protons and neutrons in some of the containers, so you may want to have some that represent 10 objects at a time so they will all fit! *Fig. 4.*

5 Punched-out paper dots work well because they don't take up much space! *Fig. 5* and *Fig. 6.*

6 Make up a game where you mix the elements up and put them back in their places or glue them to cardboard or wood to keep them in order. *Fig. 7.*

CREATIVE ENRICHMENT

Research different elements. Make a cartoon drawing of the periodic table and give each element its own personality based on its physical and chemical characteristics.

Fig. 1. Organize containers into periodic table formation.

Fig. 2. Add objects representing protons and neutrons to each element.

Fig. 4. Some elements contain more than 200 protons and neutrons, so plan ahead!

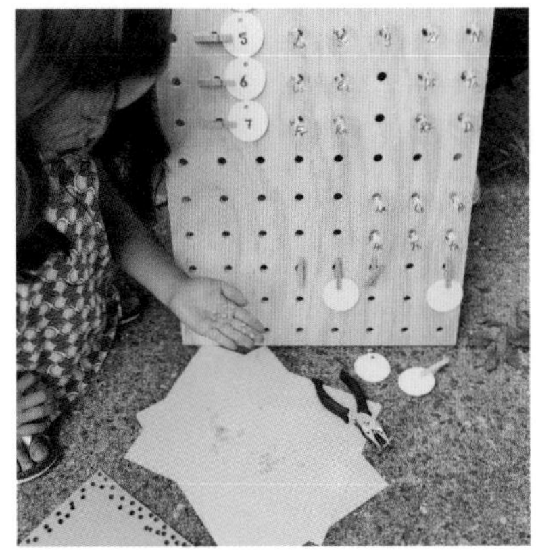
Fig. 5. Paper-punch dots make good models for protons and neutrons.

Fig. 6. Lots of paper dots fit easily in a single container.

Fig. 7. Make a game out of the table or glue the elements down.

THE STORY BEHIND THE CHEMISTRY

The ancient Greek philosopher Democritus came up with the idea for the atom over 2000 years ago, but an English schoolteacher named John Dalton solidified the theory in 1803. His atomic theory stated that matter is composed of invisible building blocks called atoms, that all the atoms of any given element are identical, and that the atoms in different elements differ in mass and behavior. He went on to state that chemical compounds are composed of two or more atoms joined together to form a molecule, and that in a chemical reaction, atoms are rearranged to form different molecules, but that no new atoms are created, and no existing atoms are destroyed. Based on these basic principles, early chemists were able to figure out the mass of different elements, based on their relative amounts in chemical compounds.

They knew from experiments that certain elements behaved in similar ways, and they started grouping these elements together.

When Mendeleev started organizing elements in order by their atomic mass, he was astonished to find that when he arranged them in horizontal lines, elements with similar chemical characteristics shared a vertical column on his new chart. Moving from left to right, he saw similar patterns from row to row. Very reactive elements ended up on the left, and unreactive elements on the right side of the table. These repeating patterns were called periods, and the periodic table was born.

The modern periodic table is based on the same principles. You'll find reactive metals on the left and unreactive nonmetals on the right. The elements headed by numbers are called "main group" elements, and those not headed by numbers are called transitions metals.

k = Ae
-Ea
RT

LAB 9

Svante August Arrhenius b. 1859

TEMPERATURE AND CHEMICAL REACTIONS

REACTIONARY CHEMIST

Born in Sweden in 1859, Svante August Arrhenius taught himself to read when he was only three and he was a mathematical prodigy. He did well in school, and by 1881 he was studying how electrical current moves through chemical solutions like salt water. Atoms or groups of atoms that hold an electrical charge are called ions, and Arrhenius was the first chemist to propose the idea that when rock salt (sodium chloride) is dissolved in water, it splits into ions: positively charged sodium atoms and negatively charged chlorine atoms that are able to carry electrical current.

BIG IDEAS

Arrhenius went on to propose that chemical reactions in solutions took place with the help of ions. In 1884 he defined the terms acids and bases, depending on what kind of ions are formed by different chemicals when you dissolve them in water. He named chemicals that produce hydrogen ions when you dissolve them in water **acids**. Chemicals that make hydroxide ions when dissolved in water were called **bases**. Later he came up with the idea that most chemical reactions have a sort of energy barrier that has to be overcome by adding heat before the reaction can occur, which he called activation energy.

NOBEL INFLUENCER

In 1900, Dr. Svante helped to establish and organize the Nobel Institutes and the Nobel Prize, using money left in the will of fellow Swede Alfred Nobel to reward those who had done work "to the greatest benefit of humankind." The first Nobel Prize was awarded in 1901, and in 1903, Svante Arrhenius became the first Swede to win a Nobel Prize in Chemistry for his work on ionic solutions. He was given membership in a number of prestigious academies of science and continued to make important contributions to science, including the study of toxins and antitoxins, and the study of carbon dioxide's effect on global temperature.

UNETHICAL BEHAVIOR

Unfortunately Arrhenius's behavior left an ugly stain on his scientific achievements. As an active board member of the Nobel Committee from 1905 until he died, he appears to have used his influence to award prizes to scientists he was friendly with and to deny them to people he didn't like. The year that Marie Curie (Lab 11) was to be awarded her Nobel Prize in Chemistry, he encouraged her to come to Stockholm in person to accept the award. When a personal scandal involving Marie broke out in the press, however, he suggested that she decline the award until the scandal cleared. Curie ignored him and traveled to Sweden to collect her well-deserved prize and deliver a lecture reasserting her claim to the discovery that radioactivity was an atomic property. Svante Arrhenius was also on the board of a Swedish institute that promoted the racist false-science of eugenics.

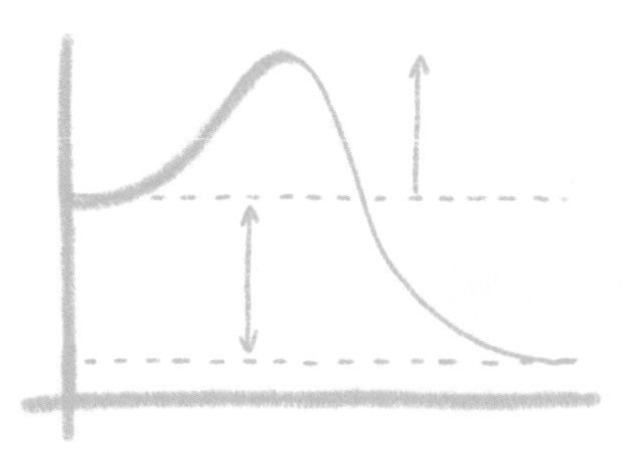

TEMPERATURE AND CHEMICAL REACTIONS

Study the difference in the reaction rate of seltzer tablets in hot water versus ice water by making chemical "lava lamps."

MATERIALS

- 2 or more tall, clear water bottles without lids
- Tray or baking sheet
- Several cups of vegetable oil
- Liquid food coloring
- Seltzer tablets
- Ice cubes

SAFETY TIPS AND HINTS

- Seltzer tablets contain medicine, so small children should be supervised when doing this project.
- Throw bottle lids away to prevent accidentally replacing them on the bottles once the seltzer tablets have been added.
- Do this once with room-temperature water to watch the chemical reaction. Then repeat with hot versus cold water to compare reaction rates.

PROTOCOL

1 Pour about two-thirds of the room-temperature water out of each bottle. *Fig. 1.*

2 Set the bottles on a tray. Fill the them almost to the top with vegetable oil, which will float on the water. Leave a few inches (5 cm) of empty air. *Fig. 2.*

3 Add several drops of food coloring to each bottle. *Fig. 3* and *Fig. 4.*

Fig. 7. Does the hot water or cold water react with the seltzer more quickly?

4 Break a seltzer tablet in half and drop both halves into the bottle to start the chemical reaction. Carbon dioxide gas will form when the seltzer dissolves in the water. *Fig. 5.*

5 Repeat the experiment but add hot water from the faucet to one bottle and ice water to the other. The water levels should be the same in each bottle. *Fig. 6.*

6 Color the hot water red and color the cold water blue. Which reaction creates carbon dioxide faster? *Fig. 7.*

CREATIVE ENRICHMENT

Chemical reactions occur in living things too. Add 1 teaspoon of yeast to ¼ cup (60 ml) of warm water in a small zip-top bag and seal it. Add 1 teaspoon of yeast to ¼ cup (60 ml) ice water in a second zipper bag. Compare how quickly the carbon dioxide from growing yeast inflates each bag. Open the bags before they explode!

Fig. 1. Pour two-thirds of the water out of a water bottle.

Fig. 2. Fill the bottles with oil, leaving space on top.

Fig. 3. Add several drops of food coloring to each bottle.

Fig. 4. Choose your favorite color.

Fig. 5. Drop a seltzer tablet into the bottle.

Fig. 6. Repeat using hot versus cold water.

THE STORY BEHIND THE CHEMISTRY

Molecules are groups of atoms held together by energetic bonds. Chemical reactions occur when molecules crash into certain other molecules under the right conditions. When this happens, bonds are broken, electrons are swapped, and new molecules are born.

Three things have to happen for chemical reactions to take place: Molecules have to collide. They have to be in the correct position, or orientation when they hit, and the collisions must have enough energy to kick off the reaction.

Arrhenius came up with an equation that used math to calculate exactly how much energy it takes for a reaction to occur and named it "activation energy." At a given temperature, the bigger the activation energy, the slower the reaction rate will be, but adding heat or light to reacting molecules can give them enough energy to overcome the activation energy barrier and react more quickly.

In this lab, we create a chemical reaction between seltzer tablets and water to produce carbon dioxide gas bubbles. Although we are not measuring how much energy it takes to activate the reaction, it is obvious that the bubbling begins much more quickly when using hot water than cold water. This happens because hot water contains more energy than cold water. In hot water, molecules move faster and collide more frequently with enough energy to activate the chemical reaction and that produces carbon dioxide bubbles.

LAB 10

Agnes Pockels b. 1862

SURFACE TENSION

KITCHEN SINK CHEMIST

Agnes Pockels was born in Venice, Italy, in 1862. Her father was an officer in the royal Austrian army, but when she was nine years old, he became very ill with malaria. Her family moved to Brunswick in Lower Saxony, which is part of Germany. Although she attended a high school for girls and was fascinated by science, women were not accepted into universities. She wanted nothing more than to continue her studies, but she was forced to remain at home to take care of her two ailing parents while her brother went off to college.

KITCHEN SINK SCIENCE

Fortunately for the field of chemistry, Agnes's curiosity was unstoppable. She began to notice interesting phenomena while washing dishes in her kitchen sink. Fascinated by how oils and particles formed films on water, she observed that those films could be disturbed by soaps and other materials. Agnes transformed her kitchen into a research station and dove into the study of surface tension, which is the name for the way molecules stick together on the surface of a fluid. Her brother Fredrich, who was studying science at the university, recognized his sister's hunger for knowledge and supported her in every way he could. Besides observing her work, he gave her access to a physics journal so that she could learn what other scientists were doing in their more well-equipped laboratories.

SLIDE TROUGH

By the time she was twenty, Agnes had invented a "slide trough," which allowed her to play with the way a liquid's surface behaved, by sliding a wire or metal strip across the top of it. She used her apparatus to create very thin layers of fluids and then to test the effect of different contaminants, such as fine powders, on surface tension. Besides discovering methods for applying uniform layers of particles to a surface, she discovered that her trough could sweep a surface free of surface contaminants.

PUBLICATION

Agnes shared her results by writing a letter to another scientist who studied the surface of liquids. He was impressed, and eventually her work was published in the famous journal *Nature*. She was delighted to learn that other scientists were using her research results and trough design in their own laboratories. Pockels continue studying surface tension, and her work led to many discoveries and innovations in surface tension research and material science.

A KIND HEART

Agnes Pockels's brother died in 1913, and following World War I her beloved physics journal was no longer published. She lived out the rest of her life in relative obscurity, always helping others. Four years before her death, Agnes was awarded the Laura R. Leonard Prize of the German Colloid Society, "for her quantitative investigation of the properties of interfaces and surface films, and for the methods she used, which have since become fundamental in modern colloid science."

SURFACE TENSION

Agnes Pockels, the founder of surface chemistry, loved science, but she was trapped in a life of domestic chores. She became interested in the surface tension of liquids while washing dishes one day and the rest is history. In this experiment, you'll use dish soap and alcohol to disrupt the surface tension of milk, water, and oil.

MATERIALS

- Small dish
- Dish soap liquid
- Plates
- Milk
- Liquid food coloring
- Cotton swabs
- Vegetable oil (or canola oil)
- Cornstarch, fine pepper, or confectionary dusting powder
- Rubbing alcohol (isopropanol) in spray bottle (optional)

SAFETY TIPS AND HINTS

If using rubbing alcohol, perform the experiment outdoors or in a well-ventilated area. Small children must be supervised. Safety goggles are recommended.

Fig. 8. Observe the changes in surface tension.

PROTOCOL

1 In a small dish, mix together some water and a large squirt of dish soap.

2 Pour a shallow layer of milk onto a plate. *Fig. 1.*

3 Add several drops of food coloring to the milk. *Fig. 2.*

4 Dip a cotton swab into the soapy water. Touch it to the surface of the milk to break the surface tension. Hold the swab in once place and observe what happens to the food coloring. *Fig. 3* and *Fig. 4.*

Fig. 1. Pour milk on a plate.

Fig. 2. Add several drops of food coloring to the milk.

Fig. 3. Touch a soapy swab to the milk to break the surface tension.

Fig. 4. Hold the swab in one place and observe what happens.

Fig. 5. Add oil to colored water.

Fig. 6. Touch a soapy swab to water, oil, and food coloring.

Fig. 7. Wearing safety glasses, spray the oil-water mixture with alcohol.

Fig. 9. Use a camera to record the movement of the fluids in slow motion.

5 Mix water and a drop of food coloring together on a new plate. Add a few small pools of oil to the plate. ***Fig. 5.***

6 Drip some food coloring into the oil and add some fine powder (optional) such as cornstarch, pepper, or dusting powder. Touch a soapy swab to the water and to the oil to see what happens. ***Fig. 6.***

Optional: Spray a mixture of food coloring, water, oil, and powder with rubbing alcohol to see what happens to the surface tension. ***Fig. 7, Fig. 8, Fig. 9.***

CREATIVE ENRICHMENT

Use a camera to record the experiment in slow motion to observe the movement of the liquids.

Study how different powders suspended on milk or water react to breaking the surface tension using dish soap.

Use different objects, such as a feather or a paper towel, to remove oil or powder from the surface of water. Will dish soap remove the oil from feathers?

Wash the dishes at your house to see how soap breaks up oil and fat in the sink.

Test different methods of physically removing oil from water.

THE STORY BEHIND THE CHEMISTRY

Water molecules love to stick together. They're called polar molecules because they have positive and negative poles like a magnet. The pole, where the two smaller hydrogen atoms hang out, is positively charged, while the oxygen end carries a small negative charge. Like weak magnets, the positive regions of water molecules are attracted to the negative regions of nearby water molecules.

If you pour liquid water onto a plate, attractive water molecules pull on each other from all directions, which keeps most of them fairly evenly spaced as they move around in the liquid. The exception is the water molecules on the surface. Because they are next to the air, nothing is pulling on them from above, so they can snuggle up to neighboring water molecules.

This packing of water molecules next to the air forms sort of an elastic skin on the surface, and the scientific name for the way the molecules stretch across the water is "surface tension." Milk is mostly made of water. In this lab, dish detergent acts as a chemical knife that breaks the surface tension on milk and water, so that food coloring and floating particles are free to swirl freely through the liquid. It's also interesting to experiment with detergent and alcohol to see how they disrupt the surface tension of a mixture of water, food coloring, and oil.

88
Ra
(226)

84
Po
(209)

LAB 11

Marie Curie b. 1867

ELEMENTAL EXTRACTION

RADIOACTIVITY PIONEER

Marie Curie, born Manya Sklodowska, entered the world in 1867 surrounded by a loving family in a house filled with laughter, books, and her father's scientific equipment. Although her childhood in Poland was filled with magical moments, challenges loomed from the start. Their lives were overshadowed by an oppressive Russian regime, which forced her father out of his academic job and the family into an apartment where they opened a boarding school to pay the bills. One of the boys who arrived to live with the family brought along body lice infected with typhus fever–causing bacteria, which killed Marie's beloved sister Zosia. Two years later, tuberculosis took her mother's life.

POLAND

The serious, gray-eyed girl took refuge in her education. By the time she was seventeen, she was actively involved in a secret "floating university," where she began to learn about chemistry and biology and dove into literature and culture. She came to believe that education was the only way to fight oppression. When she went to work as a nanny for a wealthy family, she continued to tutor the poor neighbor children, teaching them to read. Eventually she earned enough money to join her sister in Paris in 1891 to pursue her dream of attending the famous Sorbonne University.

PARIS

Marie fell in love with math and physics and soon graduated at the top of her class at the Sorbonne, despite being so preoccupied with her studies that she often forgot to eat. While searching for a home for some laboratory equipment, she met Pierre Curie, the man who would become her partner in science and in life. Together they embarked on an extraordinary adventure.

STRANGE RAYS

While pursuing her doctorate degree, Marie decided to study the strange new rays that a scientist named Becquerel had discovered emanating from the element uranium. Searching for other elements and minerals naturally emitting these rays, she discovered that uranium mining waste called pitchblende gave a stronger signal than uranium did on its own. By chemically separating the mining waste and testing each fraction, she discovered two new elements: polonium, named after her homeland, and radium. It took her four years to purify a sample of radium smaller than a grain of rice from tons of mining waste, but it was worth it when her treasured element took its place on the periodic table and she coined the word "radioactive." She could have made a small fortune by patenting her extraction method, but Marie believed that everyone should benefit from scientific discovery, so she freely shared her technique with the scientific community and industry.

RADIUM THERAPY

At first, Marie and Pierre were unaware of exactly how dangerous their discoveries were, but their fingertips were cracked from handling vials of radium, which glowed in the dark with a lovely cold blue light. After some accidental flesh burns followed by a few intentional experiments, they helped to create the first radiation therapy to target and kill cancer cells. Although radium is no longer used for radiation therapy, the technique is still used today to treat certain cancers.

TWO NOBEL PRIZES

Marie Curie went on to become the first woman to win a Nobel Prize in Physics, and later she went on to win a second Nobel in chemistry. Her curiosity, hard work, and determination changed the world and although radioactivity from her work shortened her life, she continues to inspire scientists today.

ELEMENTAL PRECIPITATION

Marie Curie coined the word "radioactivity" she is most famous for discovering the elements polonium and radium, and then developing a method for extracting radium from rocks. In this lab, you'll imitate one of the chemical reactions she used to purify radium using Epsom salts, cornstarch, and food coloring.

Fig. 5. Your fake uranium mining waste is ready for chemical processing.

MATERIALS

- Oven
- Pie tin or baking sheet
- ¼ cup (32 g) cornstarch
- ¼ cup (56 g) Epsom salt (magnesium chloride)
- Liquid food coloring, yellow and blue
- 1 tablespoon (3 g) dried rosemary leaves (optional)
- Coffee filter
- A glass for straining and a glass that holds at least 2 cups (475 ml) of liquid
- Water
- Large heatproof plate
- 1 tablespoon (15 g) washing soda (sodium carbonate) (see Resources page 121)

SAFETY TIPS AND HINTS

Washing soda is a strong base commonly used as laundry detergent. It can irritate skin and eyes, so safety glasses are recommended during washing soda steps. Small children should be supervised.

PROTOCOL

1 Set the oven to the lowest setting: 170°F (77°C). In a pie tin, mix together the cornstarch and Epsom salt. Add 1 tablespoon (15 ml) of water. Mix until you have several small clumps that look like rocks. ***Fig. 1.***

2 Drip around 5 drops of yellow food coloring and 5 drops of blue food coloring onto the mixture. ***Fig. 2.***

3 Stir briefly and spread the mixture out on the pie tin. Dry the mixture in the oven for about 1 hour, stirring every 15 minutes. When the mixture is dry, remove it from the oven and cool. ***Fig. 3.***

4 Stir in the rosemary (if using) to represent the pine needles that were mixed in with Marie Curie's uranium mining waste. ***Fig. 4*** and ***Fig. 5.***

5 Add 1 cup (235 ml) of water. Crush the cornstarch "rocks" with a spoon and stir until everything has dissolved. Skim off the rosemary that floats to the top. ***Fig. 6.***

6 Fold the edges of a coffee filter over the rim of one or two glasses and filter the solution to remove pine needles and cornstarch. Repeat until the liquid is clear. ***Fig. 7.***

7 While the Epsom salt solution filters through the paper, stir the washing soda into 1 cup (235 ml) of warm water until it dissolves. Be sure to use warm water, not hot.

Fig. 1. Combine Epsom salt, cornstarch, and water.

Fig. 2. Add food coloring to Epsom salt-cornstarch mixture.

Fig. 3. Dry mixture in the oven or air dry.

Fig. 4. Add dried rosemary to represent the pine needles mixed in with Marie Curie's uranium mining waste.

Fig. 6. Add water to dissolve cornstarch rocks and skim off pine needles.

Fig. 7. Filter through coffee filters until clear. Save green filtrate.

Fig. 8. Add green filtrate to a clear container.

Fig. 9. Slowly pour the washing soda solution into the green filtrate.

Fig. 10. Observe the chemical reaction.

Fig. 11. A white precipitate will form.

8 Pour the green filtrate into a clear container that will hold 2 cups (475 ml) of liquid. ***Fig. 8.***

9 Add the clear sodium carbonate (washing soda) solution to the green magnesium sulfate solution and observe the white magnesium carbonate precipitate that forms as a product of the chemical reaction. ***Fig. 9, Fig. 10,*** and ***Fig. 11.***

10 Spoon the white precipitate into a coffee filter over a cup and rinse it with water. Transfer the precipitate to the heatproof plate. Dry it in the oven at the lowest setting or under the oven light. ***Fig. 12.***

11 Compare the precipitate to your starting materials. ***Fig. 13.***

Fig. 12. Scoop out the precipitate and dry it out.

Fig. 13. Compare the percipitate to the starting materials.

THE STORY BEHIND THE CHEMISTRY

Marie Curie was thrilled when wagons brought tons of dusty pitchblende mining waste to her laboratory, because she knew they contained a tiny bit of an element that she had named radium. She removed dirt and pine needles, crushed the rocks, and boiled huge vats of the waste with strong acids and bases in order to collect a compound called barium sulfate, which carried radium sulfate along with it.

Dr. Curie treated the sulfate residues with sodium carbonate (washing soda) to convert them into carbonates and create a solid substance, called a precipitate. She filtered out the precipitate, washed it, and did a chemical reaction to turn the carbonates back into sulfates. She repeated the process over and over again in her quest to purify a tiny bit of pure radium.

In this lab, you create fake pitchblende mining waste using cornstarch, Epsom salts (magnesium sulfate), food coloring, and rosemary to represent the pine needles. Using a chemical reaction similar to Marie Curie's, you'll add sodium carbonate (washing soda) to convert the magnesium sulfate into magnesium carbonate and form a precipitate that won't dissolve in water. Filtering the precipitate removes most of the food coloring and water to yield a relatively pure sample of magnesium carbonate.

0 1 2 3 4 5 6 7 8 9 10 11 12 13 14

LAB 12

S. P. L. Sørensen b. 1868

THE PH SCALE

COUNTRY TO CITY

Søren Peder Lauritz Sørensen was born on a farm in Denmark in 1868. He dreamed of being a medical doctor, rather than a farmer like his father, so when he turned eighteen, he entered the University of Copenhagen. While he was there, a professor named S. M. Jorgensen convinced him to set his sights on chemistry instead of medicine and his life changed course.

INDUSTRIAL EDUCATION

As he pursued his education, Søren also worked in a chemistry laboratory at the Danish Polytechnic Institute. His skills and interests also led him to jobs outside of the university, including a geological survey of his home country of Denmark and a consulting job at the royal naval dockyard. Eventually he received a Ph.D. from the University of Copenhagen, and when he was thirty-three, Dr. Sørensen landed a job at Carlsberg Laboratory.

BREWING BETTER BEER

Carlsberg Laboratory was a brewery on a mission to brew better beer. Alcoholic beverage brewing is one of the oldest chemical industries. It utilizes the biological process of fermentation, where microorganisms such as yeast are added to grain and fruit. As they consume carbohydrates, microbes produce carbon dioxide bubbles and alcohol in the beer. At Carlberg Laboratory, Sørensen studied the chemistry of beer, and he was especially focused on learning more about the proteins in the beverage during the brewing process.

A NEW SCALE

As Sørensen studied proteins like enzymes, which are similar to chemical scissors, he noticed that how well the enzymes worked depended on how many free hydrogen atoms were in the liquid. Chemicals called acids contain lots of free hydrogen, while chemicals called bases do not. At the time, there was no way to express how many hydrogen atoms were in a certain solution. To solve this problem, Sørensen created the pH scale. The term pH means "potential of hydrogen," and the pH number is based on a mathematical scale. The more free hydrogens contained in a solution, the lower the pH number will be.

A LIFE IN THE LABORATORY

Dr. Sørensen remained at Carlsberg Laboratory for the remainder of his life. His wife Margrethe Høyrup Sørensen assisted him in much of his research, and his colleague A. J. Curtain Cosbie wrote that Sørensen "was kindly, courteous, ever-willing to listen to those who had not his fund of knowledge and always ready and glad to impart something from his vast store of learning." S. P. L. Sørensen died February 12, 1939.

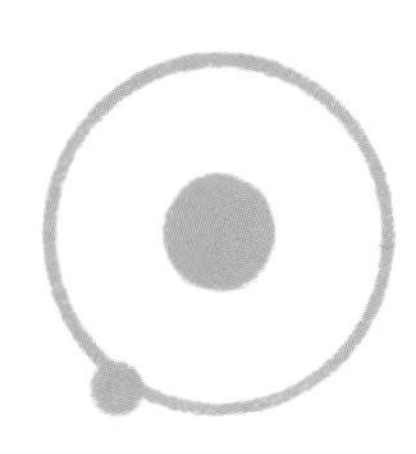

THE PH SCALE

S. P. L. Sørensen invented the pH scale, which indicates how many free hydrogen atoms are contained in a solution. In this lab, you'll make pH-indicator paint from red cabbage and from turmeric to test the pH of kitchen chemicals such as baking soda and vinegar, which can make acid-base indicators change color.

Fig. 6. Paint the flowers with baking soda solution or vinegar to see the color change.

MATERIALS

- 1 teaspoon baking soda
- 1 red or purple cabbage
- Blender
- 1 tablespoon (7 g) turmeric
- White coffee filters
- Paintbrush
- White vinegar
- Raw egg
- Small white plate or bowl

SAFETY TIPS AND HINTS

Wash your hands after handling raw eggs.

PROTOCOL

1 Add the baking soda to ¼ cup (60 ml) of water. Set it aside.

2 Chop up half of a red cabbage and put it in a blender. Cover it with water and blend. (If you don't have a blender, cook the cabbage and save the purple cooking water.) Strain out the liquid and save it. Discard the solids. ***Fig. 1*** and ***Fig. 2.***

3 Add the turmeric to ½ cup (120 ml) of water. ***Fig. 3.***

4 Use the purple cabbage juice and yellow turmeric paint to create designs on the coffee filters. ***Fig. 4.***

5 Tape painted filters to a window. You can make paper stems from coffee filters and position the stem in a small cup of water containing baking soda (step 1) or a small cup of vinegar to see what happens when capillary action pulls the liquid up the stem into the paper flower. ***Fig. 5.***

6 Alternately tape the flowers onto a window and paint them with baking soda solution (step 1) or vinegar. ***Fig. 6.***

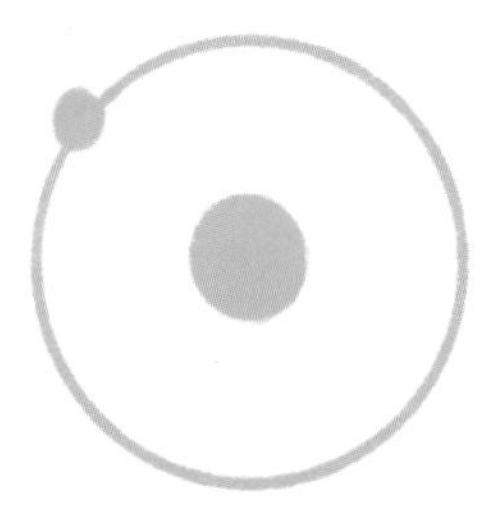

Fig. 1. Blend red cabbage in water.

Fig. 2. Strain out the liquid and save it.

Fig. 3. Mix turmeric with water.

Fig. 4. Paint designs on coffee filters and dry. Cut out flower shapes if you want to.

Fig. 5. Tape the flowers to a window with paper stems in baking soda solution or water.

CREATIVE ENRICHMENT

Use the pH-indicator paint to test other household chemicals, such as lemon juice, dish soap, and pickle juice. What else could you test?

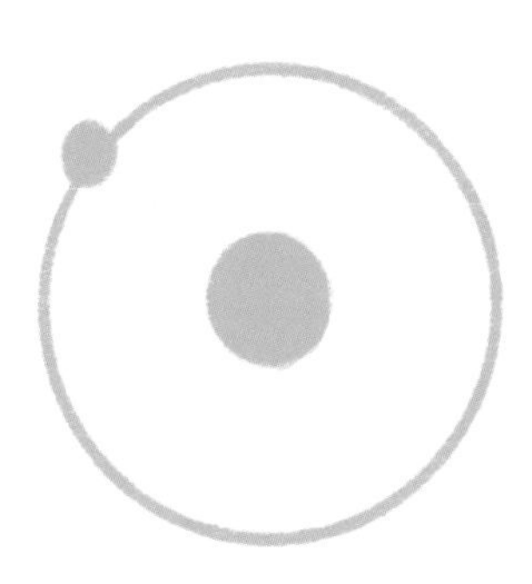

7 Test the pH of an egg white by putting it on a white plate and spattering it with cabbage juice and turmeric solution. ***Figs. 7–11.***

Fig. 7. Separate an egg white from the yolk.

Fig. 8. Sprinkle pH paint on the egg white.

Fig. 9. Observe the color change.

Fig. 10. Are egg whites acidic or basic?

Fig. 11. Photograph your egg-white experiment.

THE STORY BEHIND THE CHEMISTRY

Pigments are intensely colored molecules that absorb certain wavelengths of light and reflect others. Special pigments called acid-base indicators change color depending on whether they are exposed to an acid or a base. This happens because the pigment molecules change shape in different chemical environments and absorb light differently.

Red cabbage contains pigments called anthocyanins, which are acid-base indicators. Cabbage juice looks purple in water, which is neither an acid nor a base. However, if you add it to a solution with a high pH, the pigment will turn blue or green. In an acidic solution with a low pH, the cabbage juice will turn bright pink. Turmeric, on the other hand, is yellow in acid, and it turns dark red when it is exposed to a basic solution.

Painting baking soda and vinegar solution onto acid-base indicators lets you test whether they're acids or bases. The scientific name for vinegar is acetic acid, and it turns red cabbage pink and turmeric yellow. Baking soda is also called sodium bicarbonate. It forms a basic solution when mixed with water and turns red cabbage blue and turmeric red. See what happens when you add the pH-indicator paint to egg whites.

LAB 13

Mikhail Tsvet b. 1872

CHROMATOGRAPHY

A COLORFUL SCIENTIST

Mikhail Tsvet, whose last name means "color" in Russian, loved plants. Mikhail was born in Italy in 1872 to an Italian mother and a Russian father. The city of Asti, where he was born, is nestled between two hills. It is famous for its wine and an annual bareback horse race called the *Palio di Asti*. When Mikhail's mother died shortly after his birth, he was sent to Geneva, Switzerland, where he would spend his youth.

AN EARLY PRIZE

After receiving his undergraduate degree in math and physics, Tsvet turned his attention to botany in graduate school. His first published scientific paper brilliantly described the anatomy of plants and he was awarded the prestigious Davy Prize. In 1896 he received his Ph.D. for his work on cell physiology, which is the study of how cells function.

DO-OVER

Mikhail moved back to Russia with his father. He had to go back to school, because Swiss degrees were not recognized there, but he didn't let that obstacle slow him down. Continuing his research on plants, he taught botany classes to women at the university and eventually received a second Ph.D., which gave him the credentials to work as a laboratory assistant for fourteen years and then go on to be a professor of botany.

COLOR DRAWINGS

In 1900, Dr. Tsvet invented a new way to separate plant chemicals by moving them through a column of calcium carbonate (chalk) and he named the technique chromatography. The word chromatography is derived from the Greek word chroma and graphein. The word chroma translates to "color" and graphein means "drawing" or "writing."

In chalk chromatography, the chalk forms what is called the stationary, or unmoving phase, and the particles moving through the chalk are called the mobile, or moving, phase.

CHEMICAL SIGNATURE

As they move through chalk, smaller particles race through the column faster than large ones, leaving a signature of visible bands that can be identified and studied. The plant chemicals that Tsvet studied separated out into green, yellow, and orange bands. He was especially interested in the bands containing chlorophyll, the chemical compound that gives leaves their green hue. Although he presented his new technique to the scientific community, he died at the relatively young age of forty-seven before the importance of chromatography was recognized. Mikhail Tsvet's impact on science is still visible today, as scientists use chromatography on a regular basis in their labs.

CHROMATOGRAPHY

Use chalk and markers to study how chemical compounds like colorful pigments separate as they move through a column of chalk.

MATERIALS

- White school chalk
- Permanent or washable markers
- Shallow tray
- Rubbing alcohol (isopropanol) or water
- Paper and pencil
- Camera (optional)

SAFETY TIPS AND HINTS

Perform this experiment outdoors or in a well-ventilated area. Supervise young children around rubbing alcohol. This experiment may be performed using water and washable markers. The water method is recommended for younger children.

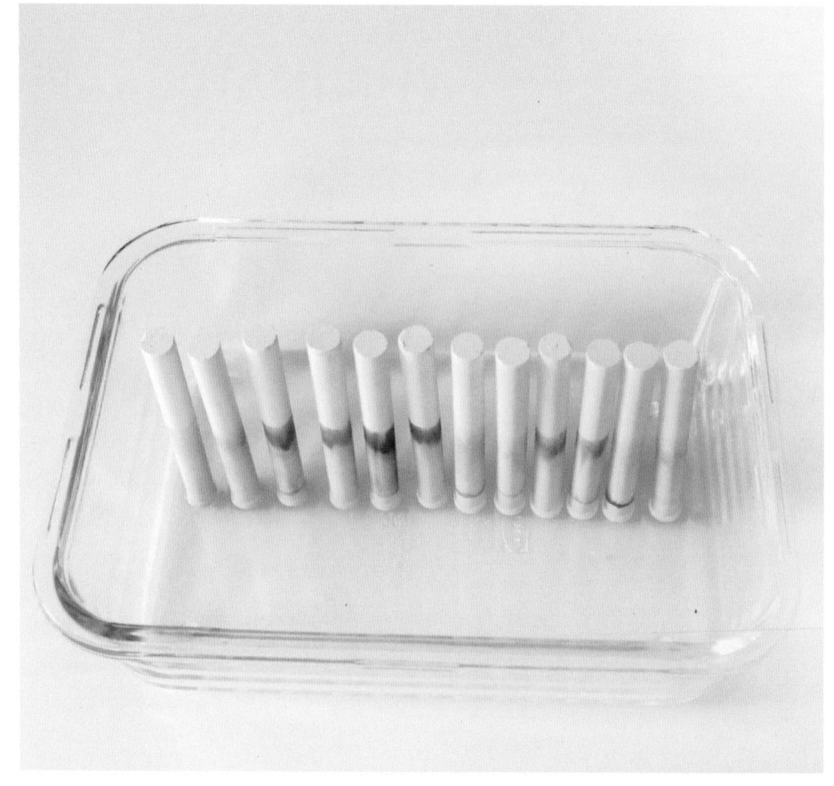

Fig. 6. Which colors separated best?

PROTOCOL

1 Draw a marker line around each piece of chalk, around ½ inch (1 cm) from the end. Use one color per piece of chalk. Green, orange, brown, pink, purple, and black work well. ***Fig. 1.***

2 Set the chalk on end in a shallow tray or dish. The end with the marker line should be closest to the tray. Record the beginning colors and guess what colors will separate from each of them. ***Fig. 2.***

3 If using permanent markers, add a shallow layer of rubbing alcohol to the tray. It should not come up to the line on the chalk. If using washable marker, add water to the tray. ***Fig. 3.***

4 Observe what happens as the liquid moves up the chalk. ***Fig. 4.***

5 Let the alcohol or water move up the chalk column until the colors have separated. Take photos every few minutes to record the changes. ***Fig. 5.***

6 Note which colors separated best and how many colors you could see in each. Were your guesses correct? ***Fig. 6.***

CREATIVE ENRICHMENT

Try this experiment using natural pigments by using a coin to press a line of plant color onto the bottom of a strip of paper made from a coffee filter. Tape the strip of paper onto a pencil and dangle the end near the plant color into rubbing alcohol so that the plant pigment is separated as it moves up the paper. Fall leaves or spinach leaves work well.

Fig. 1. Draw marker lines around the pieces of chalk.

Fig. 2. Set the chalk on end in a shallow dish.

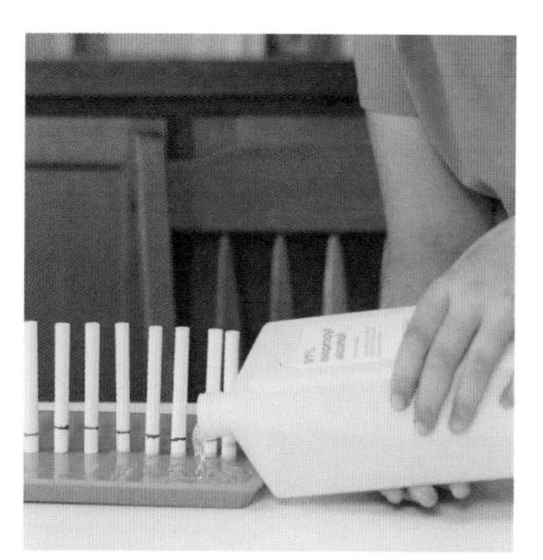
Fig. 3. Add a shallow layer of alcohol to the tray or dish.

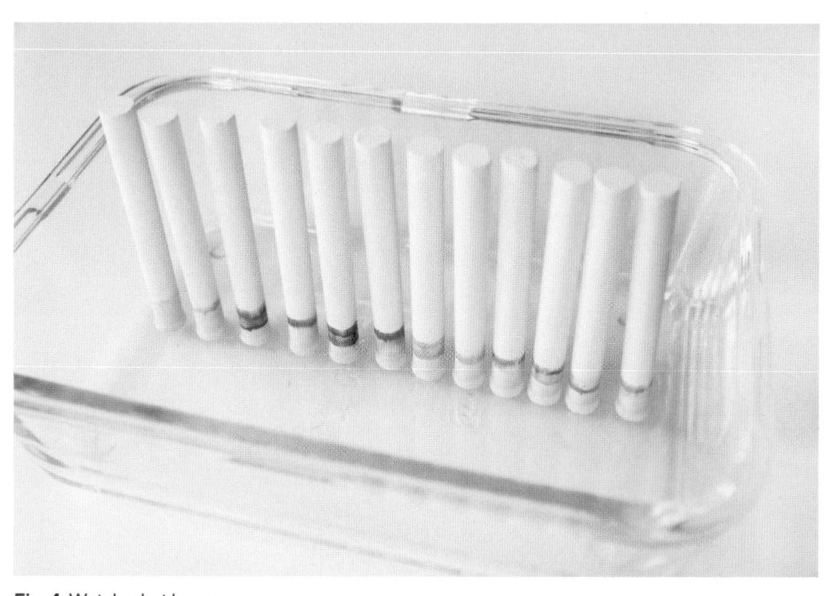
Fig. 4. Watch what happens.

Fig. 5. Observe the separating pigments and photograph them.

THE STORY BEHIND THE CHEMISTRY

In this lab, liquid climbs up the tiny spaces between the particles of calcium carbonate in chalk. Alcohol is a chemical called a solvent, which dissolves the chemicals in the permanent ink. As it travels up the column of chalk, the fluid pulls the ink up with it.

Colorful chemicals, called pigments, race ahead with small pigments at the leading edge as large pigments follow more slowly. They struggle to navigate the spaces in the chalk and soon visible bands of different colors appear. Certain shades, such as black and brown, are made by mixing several colors together, and it is fun to discover which distinctive colors make up other hues, such as green and purple.

Plants contain a number of colorful pigments, including green chlorophyll and red, purple, pink, and blue anthocyanins. (Lab 12) In the fall, many leaves stop making green chlorophyll. Red, yellow, and orange pigments can be separated using paper chromatography, which is similar to chalk chromatography.

LAB 14

Alice Ball b. 1892

ORGANIC OIL EXTRACTION

FAMILY OF ARTISTS

Born in 1892 in Seattle, Alice Ball was exposed to chemistry at a very young age. Her grandfather was a famous photographer and one of the first people in the United States to take daguerreotype images, which required the use of iodine, copper, and mercury. Sadly, her grandfather was ill, possibly as a result of chemical exposure, and Alice's family moved to Hawaii for a year in hopes that the sunny climate and sea air would improve his health. When he died, they returned to Seattle, where Alice received degrees in pharmaceutical chemistry and pharmacy from the University of Washington.

HAWAII

For graduate school, Alice chose to attend the University of Hawaii, where she became the first woman and the first African American to earn a master's degree in chemistry at the school. For her graduate thesis, Alice separated out the chemical parts of kava root, in order to discover its active components. Harry Hollman, an assistant surgeon at a nearby hospital, heard about her work on kava root and asked her to help solve the problem of treating Hansen's disease, which is also called leprosy. A leper colony had been established on the Hawaiian island of Molokai in 1865, and thousands of Hawaiians with the disease had been sent there in an attempt to stop the spread of the disease.

A NEW TREATMENT FOR LEPROSY

As a professor at the University of Hawaii, Ball devoted every moment that she wasn't teaching to synthesizing a better treatment for the disfiguring disease. At the time, the only way to reduce the symptoms of Hansen's disease was to inject or swallow chaulmoogra oil, which had been extracted from the seeds of a type of evergreen tree. Unfortunately the oil didn't work well. Painful injections formed a necklace of blisters under the skin that weren't easily absorbed by the patient's bodies, and the oil tasted so horrible it was impossible to drink without vomiting. In only a year, twenty-three-year-old Professor Ball figured out how to separate the oil into parts until she found a compound that could be extracted and made into an easily absorbable medicine for victims of Hansen's disease.

STOLEN WORK

Tragically, Alice Ball died when she was only twenty-four years old, soon after making her discovery. She may have died from exposure to chlorine gas during a lab demonstration, but it is unclear. Her death certificate was altered to state that she died of tuberculosis. The university's president, who was also a chemist, took over Ball's studies, publishing her results under his own name, and producing large quantities of the medicine she'd created.

AN ALLY

When he realized what had happened, Harry Hollman made it public that credit for Alice Ball's discovery had been stolen by the president of the university. Hollman published a paper of his own, crediting Alice for her work and dubbing her leprosy treatment the "Ball Method." Until effective antibiotics were invented in the 1940s, Alice Ball's treatment was the only effective medicine for Hansen's disease. Recently the University of Hawaii erected a plaque in her honor, awarded her a medal, and named a scholarship after her. The state of Hawaii now celebrates "Alice Ball Day."

ORGANIC OIL EXTRACTION

Extract oil from orange peels, and separate it from the juice and water using an eyedropper or syringe. Compare it to other oils in your kitchen.

Fig. 1. Squeeze oranges and save the juice to drink.

MATERIALS

- 20 oranges
- Orange juicer
- Scissors
- Large cooking pot
- Colander
- Garlic press, potato ricer, or sieve
- Thermometer
- Small bowl
- Eyedropper or syringe
- Jar

SAFETY TIPS AND HINTS

- To collect more oil, use more oranges and scoop out the white pith after juicing the oranges. Most of the oil is in the skin of the fruit, near the surface.
- Store essential orange oil in the refrigerator for up to three months.

PROTOCOL

1 Squeeze the oranges and save the fresh-squeezed juice to drink. Save the peels. To get more oil, scrape out the white pith. (Optional) ***Fig. 1*** and ***Fig. 2.***

2 Cut the peels into pieces small enough to fit in a garlic press. ***Fig. 3.***

3 Add the peels to the cooking pot. Cover with water, and warm to 110°F (43°C). Turn off the heat and drain the peels in a colander, pressing gently with your hands to remove excess water. ***Fig. 4.***

4 Press oil from the peels using a garlic press, potato ricer, or sieve. Collect the oil in a bowl. ***Fig. 5.***

5 Use an eyedropper or syringe to collect the oil floating on top of the liquid. Alternately freeze the liquid and pour off the oil. ***Fig. 6.***

6 Store your oil in a jar in the refrigerator. Use it as flavoring for food, scent for soap (Lab 2) or natural insect repellent. ***Fig. 7.***

7 Compare the orange oil to other oils in your house, including olive oil, coconut oil, and vegetable oil. Which oils are liquid at room temperature? Which oils remain liquid in the refrigerator?

CREATIVE ENRICHMENT

Extract citrus oil such as orange oil or lemon oil using the evaporation method in Lab 1.

Fig. 2. Keep the peels.

Fig. 3. Use scissors to cut the peels into small pieces.

Fig. 4. Warm peels to 110°F (43°C) and drain.

Fig. 5. Press out the oil and collect in a bowl.

Fig. 6. Collect the oil using a syringe or eyedropper.

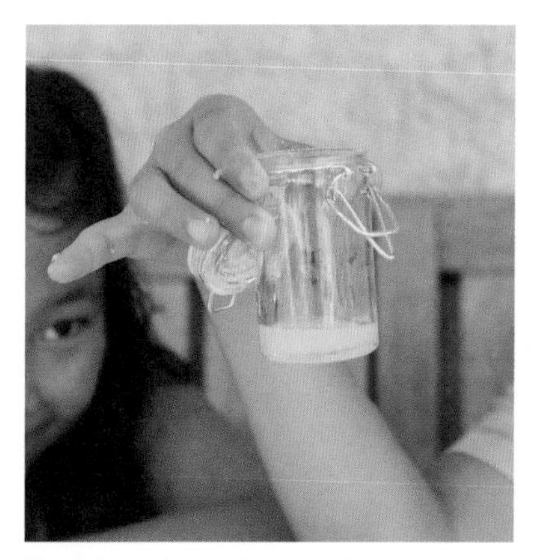
Fig. 7. Store essential orange oil in a jar.

THE STORY BEHIND THE CHEMISTRY

Before therapeutic oils can be fractionated into their parts and studied by scientists like Dr. Ball, they must be extracted from plants. One method of extracting essential oils from plants is called cold pressing, which is a mechanical method. Rather than using high heat and condensation to collect oils, the cold-press method requires that plants be crushed and squeezed until the oil is expressed. Then the oil can be separated from the other liquids that are squeezed out.

Most of the essential oils in citrus plants are contained in the fruit peels, near the surface. A colorless liquid called limonene is the major component of the oils found in citrus peels. It belongs to a group of chemical compounds called terpenes, which plants produce in order to repel pests. Most people consume some limonene on a regular basis, because it is added to a number of foods and beverages to add citrus flavor. Limonene is also contained in many "natural" insect repellents.

Because fractionating essential oils in order to study them more closely isn't easy to do at home, this lab focuses on the first step: collecting oil using a cold-press method. Once you've collected your oil, use it to add scent to soap (Lab 2) or flavor a dessert. You can even rub it on your skin to see whether it keeps mosquitos away.

LAB 15

Gerty Cori b. 1896

THE CORI CYCLE

SETTING SAIL

Named after a transatlantic ship, Gerty Theresa Cori was born in Prague in 1896. Her father was a chemist who directed a sugar refinery, and she was tutored at home by her mother until she was ten and began attending the local school for girls. By the time she was sixteen, Gerty had decided that she wanted to be a medical doctor, but discovered that she lacked many of the classes that were required. She worked extremely hard and in the course of a year learned the science, language, and math she would need to study medicine. Her uncle, who was a professor of pediatrics, encouraged her to apply to medical school and she was admitted to a university in Prague.

A LAB PARTNER

While she was in medical school, Gerty met Carl Cori, who thought that she was smart and funny. They both loved the outdoors and working in a laboratory. After finishing medical school, they married and Gerty went to work in a laboratory at a children's hospital, where she did research on thyroid disease in children. In 1922 they moved to the United States, where they hoped Gerty wouldn't be discriminated against on the basis of her Jewish heritage. They became U.S. citizens and went to work together in a research at what is now the Roswell Park Comprehensive Cancer Center in New York.

THE CORI CYCLE

A director at the Roswell Research Institute, who didn't like having women in the laboratory, tried his best to get rid of Gerty, but Carl stood up for her and she refused to leave. Despite the hostile environment, the Coris worked together day and night to study how the human body turns carbohydrates into energy. In 1929, they proposed a "cycle of carbohydrates" in which a sugar called glucose in muscles is cleaved into lactic acid, which the liver can turn back into glucose for muscles to utilize again. Gerty was listed as the first author on the papers related to this work, and today that cycle is named after her and Carl. Eventually, the Coris moved to Washington University in St. Louis, where they continued their research. Gerty returned to her love of pediatric medicine by studying metabolic disorders in children.

A NOBEL PRIZE

In 1945 Gerty Cori became the first American woman, and the third woman ever, to win a Nobel Prize in science when she and Carl were awarded the Nobel Prize for Physiology or Medicine for their work on the Cori cycle. Sadly, like Marie Curie and Irene Curie who also won Nobel prizes, Dr. Cori's early death was probably the result of radiation exposure. Her contributions to science are foundational to scientific research that continues today.

THE CORI CYCLE

Use a colorful acid-base indicator to illustrate how the Cori cycle takes lactic acid from fatigued muscles to the liver, where it turned back into glucose and returned to muscles via the bloodstream.

MATERIALS

- ½ head of red or purple cabbage
- Saucepan or pot
- Knife
- 3 clear containers, such as glasses
- 1 teaspoon baking soda
- ¼ cup (60 ml) white vinegar
- Paper towels

SAFETY TIPS AND HINTS

- Use adult supervision when chopping cabbage.
- You may have to add a little bit more baking soda (⅛ teaspoon [0.5 g]) to the center "liver" cup, if the cabbage juice is still pink when it reaches the final "muscle" cup. It should be purple again.

Fig. 7. The color change represents how the liver changes lactic acid back into glucose and returns it to the muscles.

PROTOCOL

1 Chop up half a head of red cabbage. Add it to a pot, cover it with water, and boil for 5 minutes. Cool, strain out the cabbage, and save the purple juice. ***Fig. 1.***

2 Add ½ cup (120 ml) of cabbage juice to one clear cup and label it "exercising muscle." Imagine that the purple color represents glucose in the muscle. ***Fig. 2.***

3 In a second cup, mix the baking soda with ½ cup (120 ml) water and label the cup "liver," to represent the liver. ***Fig. 3.***

4 Position a third cup on the end and label it "muscle." The liver cup should be between the two muscle cups.

5 Imagine that the exercising muscle is getting tired and lactic acid is building up inside. Add the vinegar (an acid) to the exercising muscle cup to represent lactic acid. The acid will turn the cabbage juice pink. ***Fig. 4.***

6 Fold half a paper towel in half the long way and in half again to make a long strip. Repeat with a second half paper towel. Fold them in half the long way and trim the ends so that they will hang comfortably between the three containers. These towels with represent blood vessels.

7 Position the first paper towel between the "exercising muscle" and the "liver" cups. Place the second one between the "liver" and "muscle" cups. ***Fig. 5.***

8 Observe what happens. A force called capillary action will pull the liquid up the paper towels, from cup to cup until all three cups contain the same volume of liquid. ***Fig. 6.***

9 Eventually the chemical reaction in the "liver" cup turns the liquid that travels to the "muscle" cup purple again, representing how the liver changes lactic acid back into glucose for muscles to use as energy. ***Fig. 7.***

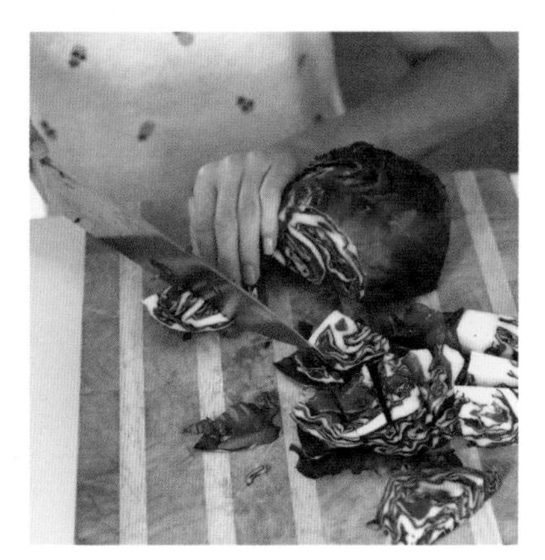
Fig. 1. Chop red cabbage.

Fig. 2. Add ½ cup (120 ml) cabbage juice to one cup.

Fig. 3. Label a second cup "liver" and add baking soda and water.

Fig. 4. Add ¼ cup (60 ml) vinegar to the "exercising muscle" cup to represent lactic acid.

Fig. 5. Use the paper towels to make bridges between the cups.

Fig. 6. Watch what happens.

CREATIVE ENRICHMENT

Next time you're exercising and feel your muscles cramp from lactic acid build-up, remember that your liver will come to the rescue and send new glucose soon.

THE STORY BEHIND THE CHEMISTRY

The human body is good at recycling energy. Our muscles primarily depend on a sugar called glucose for the energy they need. During intense exercise, muscles can become oxygen-starved and turn to a different pathway for processing energy. This causes a substance called lactic acid to build up.

Lactic acid is sent to the liver via the bloodstream, where it undergoes a process called gluconeogenesis which recycles it back into glucose. The glucose is then returned to muscles or stored as chemical energy. In this lab, we use color change to illustrate how the Cori cycle works.

Cabbage juice changes color depending on its pH (see Lab 12.) Adding acidic vinegar to the "muscle cup" turns the solution pink to represent acid build-up. A paper towel carries liquid to the "liver" cup containing baking soda that will turn it blue or purple, showing a second chemical change. Finally a paper towel carries the liquid to a third cup, to represent the return of glucose to the muscles.

LAB 16

Maria Goeppert-Mayer b. 1906

THE NUCLEAR SHELL MODEL

AN EDUCATION

Atoms are the building blocks of matter. Maria Goeppert-Mayer is best known for discovering how the spinning of protons and neutrons inside of atoms affects the structure of the nucleus and the stability of different elements. Born in 1906, Goeppert-Mayer grew up in Germany admiring her father, a sixth-generation professor of pediatrics who understood the importance of educating women. Although the preparatory school for girls she attended closed down, Maria and four other girls continued to study and were able to pass their exams for acceptance into the university.

JUMPING ELECTRONS

Germany needed teachers for girls' schools and Maria Goeppert had planned to study math in college, but she found herself irresistibly drawn to physics and pursued a Ph.D. in that discipline. Maria loved graduate school and had three Nobel-winning physicists on her committee. In her doctoral paper, she described a theory called two-photon absorption that correctly predicted that bundles of energy called photons can make electrons jump to higher energy levels.

COMING TO AMERICA

In 1930, Goeppert married another scientist named Joseph Mayer and amended her name to Maria Goeppert-Mayer. They moved to Baltimore, Maryland, in the United States, where Joseph had been offered a job at Johns Hopkins University. Maria was not offered a job, because there was an outdated rule against hiring spouses, which had become an excuse not to hire women as professors. They gave her a job writing letters in German, and in return she got a tiny salary along with access to a lab where she could continue her research. She also got to teach a few classes, but was not paid.

PHYSICS "FOR THE FUN OF IT"

After being fired from John Hopkins in 1937, Joseph went to work at Columbia University and Maria was given an office there but no salary. Still unpaid, but determined to pursue her work, Goeppert-Mayer continued her research for the sheer pleasure of doing physics. At Columbia she became friends with the famous physicist Enrico Fermi and did some work on the electron shells of radioactive transuranic elements, which are elements with atomic numbers larger than 92.

MANHATTAN TO CHICAGO

Shortly after beginning her first paid teaching position at Sarah Lawrence College, Dr. Goeppert-Mayer was recruited to work on the Manhattan Project, which eventually produced the world's first atomic bombs and brought World War II to an end. She and Joseph moved to Chicago, where he was employed as a professor by the University of Chicago and she was offered a position as a "voluntary" associate professor. Soon she was offered a part-time job as a senior physicist at the nearby Argonne National Laboratory.

A WALTZ

It was in Chicago that Goeppert-Meyer did her Noble Prize–winning research on the structure of the nuclei of atoms. She liked to describe nuclei as concentric circles of waltzing couples, some spinning clockwise and others counterclockwise while the couples twirl "round and round." In 1960 Maria Goeppert-Meyer finally became a full professor. In 1963 she shared a Nobel Prize with J. Hans D. Jensen and Eugene Paul Wigner for her discoveries concerning nuclear shell structure, becoming the second woman in history to win a Nobel Prize in Physics.

LOOKING INSIDE THE ATOM

While Maria Goeppert-Mayer studied protons and neutrons inside the nucleus, you can visualize the electrons outside the nucleus by building a Bohr model.

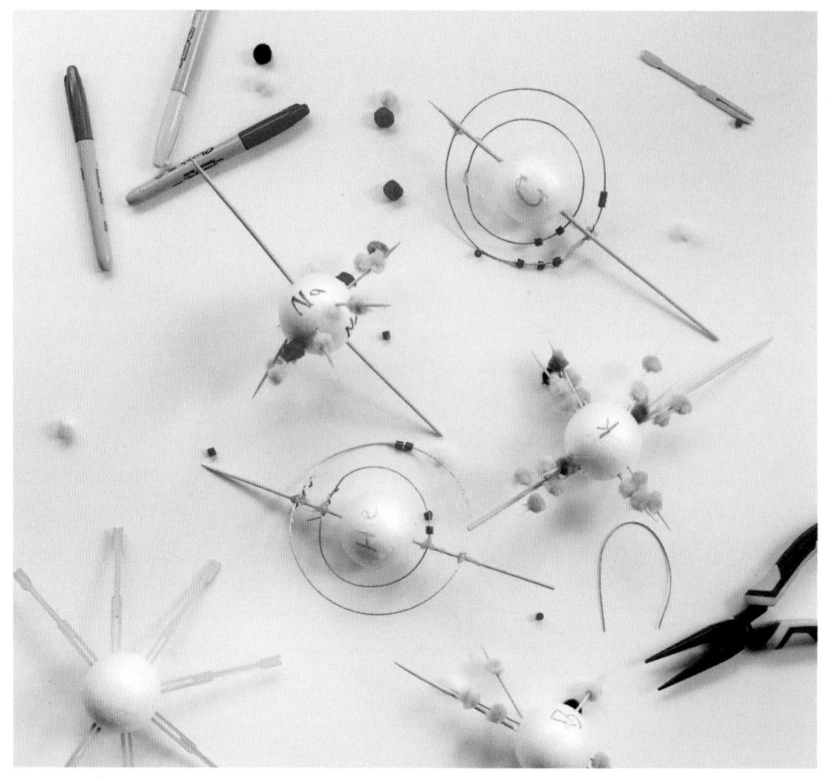

Fig. 6. Compare electron shells of different elements.

MATERIALS

- Periodic table of elements
- Toothpicks
- Skewers
- Wire (optional)
- Styrofoam balls
- Beads, small pom-poms, or other small round objects
- Hot glue or school glue

SAFETY TIPS AND HINTS

Supervise small children with toothpicks, skewers, and hot glue guns.

PROTOCOL

1 Choose an element to represent by searching online or using the periodic table (page 122). The element's atomic number will tell you how many protons and electrons the element contains. *Fig. 1.*

2 To figure out the number of neutrons in the element, subtract the number of protons from element's atomic mass.

3 Look up the electron arrangement for the element you chose. *Fig. 2.*

4 Write down how many protons, neutrons, and electrons the element contains.

Use skewers, toothpicks ,or wire (if using) to create scaffolding for electrons on a Styrofoam ball nucleus. *Fig. 3.*

5 Add bead or pom-pom electrons to the model. Position electrons in orbital shells around the nucleus, or create a random cloud of electrons. *Fig. 4.*

6 Put the atoms on a skewer to make a chemistry puppet show or a bouquet of atoms. *Fig. 5.*

7 Compare the electron shells of the different elements. *Fig. 6.*

CREATIVE ENRICHMENT

Figure out some new ways to represent an atom. Could you use a balloon? Hula Hoops? Fruit? Candy?

Fig. 1. Look up the atomic structure of an element online or on the periodic table.

Fig. 2. Find the electron arrangement for the element.

Fig. 3. Make scaffolding for the electrons.

Fig. 4. Arrange the electrons around the nucleus.

Fig. 5. Make a puppet show or atomic bouquet.

THE STORY BEHIND THE CHEMISTRY

Dr. Goeppert-Mayer's Nobel Prize-winning research on the structure of atomic nuclei added an essential layer of understanding to earlier scientific discoveries about the structure of atoms and their electron shells. Before Ernest Rutherford presented his model of the atom in 1911, scientists were just beginning to discover tools for dissecting the invisible word of the atom. They had no idea that atoms contained a concentrated central core of electrical charge, which we now call a nucleus.

In fact, early scientists thought atoms were sort of like "plum pudding" consisting of negatively charged particles called electrons floating around in a positively charged cloud. That theory changed when Rutherford famously aimed radioactive alpha particles at a sheet of gold foil in 1909. Instead of passing easily through the wispy theoretical cloud of scattered protons and electrons as predicted, a few of them hit something massive and bounced back at Rutherford. He had discovered the nucleus.

Not long afterward, in 1913, Rutherford and Niels Bohr presented a "shell" model of an atom called the Bohr model, with a central nucleus surrounded by rings of orbiting electrons. Over the last century, scientists have come to understand that atoms are mostly empty space. In atoms, electrons exist in electron clouds around the nucleus, moving too unpredictably for us to know their location at any given time.

In this lab, you can choose to make an atom with a cloud of electrons or a Bohr model. The Bohr model makes it easier to visualize electrons in their different energy states, with some closer to the nucleus and others farther away.

Rachel Carson b. 1907

DISPERSION OF ENVIRONMENTAL CONTAMINANTS

ENVIRONMENTAL WARRIOR

Born in 1907 Rachel Carson was a lifelong nature lover and student of science. After studying to be a marine biologist, she ended up working as a writer for the United States Department of Fish and Wildlife. Her lyrical books on the ocean's geology and ecosystems led the American public to fall in love with science and made her one of the most popular science writers of her time.

A NEW PESTICIDE

Carson's job at the Department of Fish and Wildlife made her a witness to some of the first reports about the devastating effects the new "wonder" pesticide DDT was having on fish and wildlife populations. As she studied the data, it became clear to her that the chemical was killing more than mosquitos and other insects. Her background in chemistry and biology helped her understand that DDT had traveled through soil and water from the fields and wetlands where it had been sprayed, into nearby lakes, streams, and rivers. The pesticide had then made its way up the food chain from invertebrates into the bodies of fish, birds, and mammals.

SILENT SPRING

Carson wasn't the only one that noticed the declining wildlife populations. After the government started spraying the chemical regularly around the United States, many people noticed the gradual disappearance of birds and missed their song in springtime.

DAVID AND GOLIATH

In 1962 Rachael Carson sparked the environmental movement. Understanding the significance of the chemical threat she was witnessing, Rachael wrote her famous book, *Silent Spring*, using scientific evidence to support her claim that DDT was harming ecosystems. She stood up to the huge chemical corporations that were producing the chemical and telling the public that it was safe. She made the argument that the chemicals we use in the environment will eventually reappear in our own bodies. Her words and her bravery resulted in the ban of the pesticide DDT in the United States.

THE ENVIRONMENTAL MOVEMENT

Even before writing *Silent Spring*, Rachael Carson reminded readers that what we do to the environment, we do to ourselves. Small in stature and unmarried, she was bullied, ridiculed, and criticized for her writing. She was called "a spinster," "hysterical," and "an uninformed woman speaking of that which she did not know." Nevertheless, she persisted and DDT was banned. Rachel Carson refused to be silent. She used her words, her voice, and her education in science to save the things she loved. In doing so, she sparked the environmental movement that continues today.

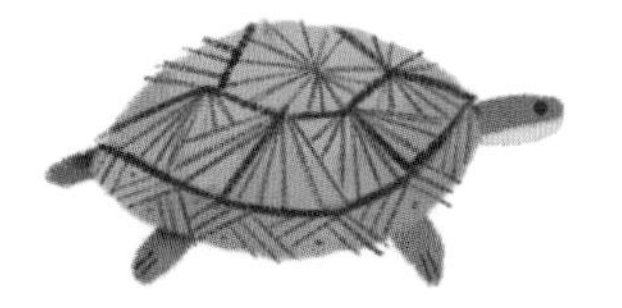

DISPERSION OF ENVIRONMENTAL CONTAMINANTS

In 1962 biologist Rachel Carson raised the alarm that the chemical insecticide DDT was spreading through the soil of fields and forests where it had been sprayed, to nearby waterways, killing fish and birds in addition to insects. This lab lets you observe food coloring as it moves through a field of gelatin into nearby water.

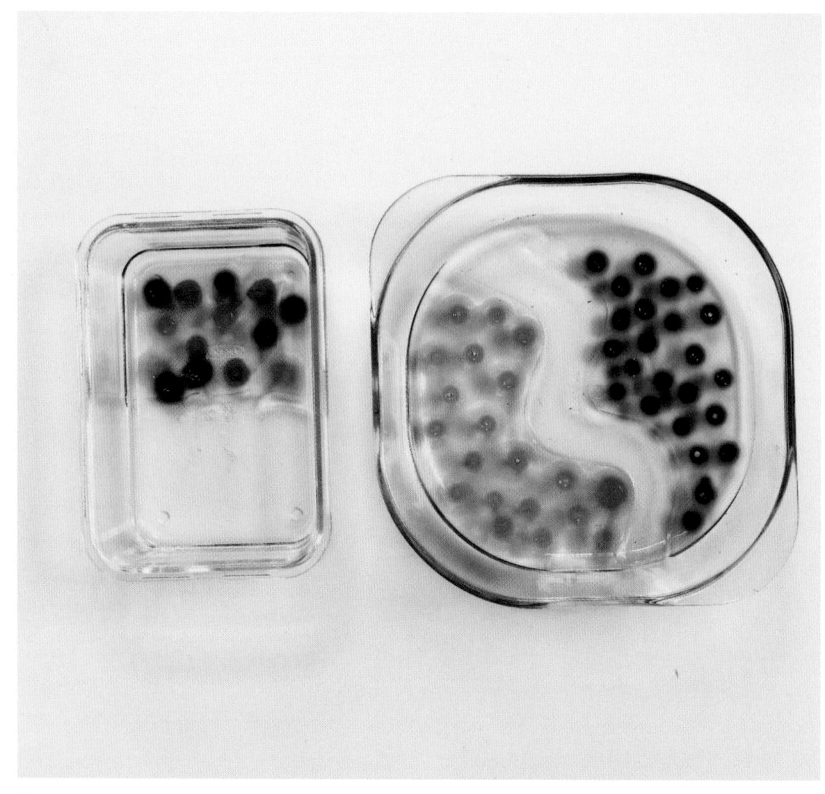

Fig. 6. Carefully fill the "lake" or "stream" carved in the gelatin with water.

MATERIALS

- 4 cups (940 ml) water
- 4 (1-ounce [28 g]) envelopes of plain gelatin
- Medium-sized glass casserole dish
- Table knife
- Compostable plastic straws or plastic straws
- Toothpicks or skewers (if needed)
- Liquid food coloring

SAFETY TIPS AND HINTS

Adult supervision is required with hot water and gelatin.

PROTOCOL

1 Bring the water to a boil in the microwave or on the stove. Add the plain gelatin and stir until completely dissolved, reheating if needed. *Fig. 1.*

2 Allow the gelatin to cool to a safe temperature and pour it into the casserole dish until it is around 1 inch (2.5 cm) thick. Let it solidify at room temperature or in the refrigerator. *Fig. 2.*

3 Use a table knife to cut a lake or stream into the gelatin, leaving a large area of undisturbed gelatin in the container. Remove the gelatin from the lake or stream area so you can fill it with water later. *Fig. 3.*

4 Poke one end of a straw into the gelatin, but not all the way through, to create a hole. Twist the straw and remove the gelatin plug. If it doesn't come out, use a toothpick or skewer to get the plug out of the hole. *Fig. 4.*

5 Repeat to create a series of holes in the gelatin. Add a drop of food coloring to each hole. Use all four colors, or if you've created a river space, add blue to the holes on one side and yellow to the holes on the other side. *Fig. 5.*

6 Place the experiment in a spot where it won't be disturbed and carefully pour water into the lake or stream you created so that it's just below the top surface of the gelatin and won't overflow into the food coloring. *Fig. 6.*

7 Observe the food coloring over the next several days as it moves through the gelatin and into to the water. If the river or stream water is evaporating, carefully add a little bit more water to bring it to its original level.

Fig. 1. Add gelatin to water.

Fig. 2. Pour melted gelatin into a glass container.

Fig. 3. Cut a "lake" or "stream" into the gelatin.

Fig. 4. Use a straw to poke holes in the gelatin.

Fig. 5. Add food coloring to each of the holes.

CREATIVE ENRICHMENT

Change the temperature of the experiment to see how chemicals might disperse more quickly or slowly in summer or winter.

Embed a strip of living of wheatgrass into the gelatin shoreline to see how plants with long roots can slow the progression of chemicals into a waterway.

Use perfume to test how chemicals disperse through air.

THE STORY BEHIND THE CHEMISTRY

Insecticides are chemicals designed to kill invertebrate pests, such as insects. Ideally, they kill their targets without harming humans or other animals, but this isn't always the case. DDT, the most effective insecticide the world had ever seen, was developed in 1939.

DDT

In 1945, DDT became available in the United States and dead birds began to appear in areas where it had been sprayed. Rachael Carson used science to demonstrate that the chemical was moving through soil, water and the food chain to cause cellular and genetic damage in many living things.

CHEMICAL DISPERSION

Chemicals can spread from areas where they are packed tightly together in high concentrations, to areas of lower concentration. This type of movement, called dispersion, can take place in gases like air, liquids like water and solids, like the compounds that make up soil. This is a problem when toxic chemicals move away from the spot where they've been applied. This lab demonstrates how chemicals can move into a pond or stream.

LAB 18

Anna Jane Harrison b. 1912

ORGANIC COMPOUNDS AND ULTRAVIOLET LIGHT

ONE-ROOM SCHOOLHOUSE

Anna Jane Harrison grew up on a farm in Missouri. When she asked her father about caterpillars, he taught her about the tractors instead of the butterfly larvae. She tucked the memory away as her earliest brush with science. When he died in 1919, her mother continued running the farm to support seven-year-old Anna and her brother. Anna loved going to school in a one-room schoolhouse, and was inspired by her wonderful teacher there.

TEACHING

She attended college and graduate school at the University of Missouri, studying chemistry and education, and she taught at the one-room school house that she had attended as she worked toward her master's degree. In 1940, she finished her Ph.D. in physical chemistry. She went to work teaching chemistry at a women's college in New Orleans.

SMOKE DETECTOR

During World War II, Anna took a break from teaching and went to work doing research for the government. In a lab in Kansas City, Missouri, she studied toxic smoke for the National Defense Research Committee and did some work at Corning Glass Works in New York. Some of the work she did resulted in the invention of smoke detectors.

LIGHT WORK

Dr. Harrison joined the faculty at Mount Holyoke College in Massachusetts to work with Emma P. Carr, an expert on ultraviolet spectroscopy, a laboratory technique that uses light waves to analyze chemicals. In addition to using spectroscopy to study chemicals, Harrison used a technique called flash photolysis to break organic chemicals apart. As the reaction happened, she used spectroscopy to see what chemical fragments were created and whether they interacted with each other. She was especially interested in how organic compounds, which contain carbon linked to other elements, interact with ultraviolet light.

PUBLIC EDUCATION

Anna's students loved her. Besides having a good sense of humor, she was able to communicate complicated concepts in terms that everyone could understand. Dr. Harrison felt that it was essential for the public and policy makers to have a basic understanding of science, so that they could make decisions that would benefit everyone. She worked with a number of science organizations to help communicate science to the public, including the National Science Foundation, the National Science Board, and the American Chemical Society.

TRAVELING FOR SCIENCE

In 1978 Anna Harrison became the first female president of the American Chemical Society, and in 1983 she was named president of the American Association for the Advancement of Science. Her work as a scientist and a science educator gave her the opportunity to travel around the world. She visited India, Thailand, Japan, and Spain as part of her mission to improve the way scientists talk to each other and communicate with the public. Dr. Harrison died in Massachusetts in 1998 when she was eighty-five years old.

ORGANIC COMPOUNDS AND ULTRAVIOLET LIGHT

In this lab, you will take advantage of the ultraviolet rays in sunlight to break down the organic dye molecules in construction paper to fade it out—creating sun prints.

Fig. 7. The ultraviolet rays will fade the dye in the paper where it wasn't protected from the sunlight.

MATERIALS

- Brightly colored construction paper
- Scissors
- Plastic wrap
- Stencil (optional)

SAFETY TIPS AND HINTS

This project works best in direct sunlight when the sun is almost directly overhead.

PROTOCOL

1 Cut shapes out of colored construction paper or card stock. *Fig. 1.*

2 Put the shapes on top of a second piece of colorful paper. *Fig. 2.*

3 Find a sunny spot to make your sun print. *Fig. 3.*

4 Cover the paper with plastic wrap, and weigh it down with rocks if it's a windy day. *Fig. 4.*

5 A stencil also works well for this project. *Fig. 5.*

6 After several hours in direct sunlight, remove the top paper to reveal your sun print. *Fig. 6.*

7 The ultraviolet rays in sunlight will fade the organic dyes in the paper, leaving a darker image where it was protected by paper. *Fig. 7.*

CREATIVE ENRICHMENT

Repeat this experiment by comparing how ultraviolet rays fade paper in shade versus direct sunlight on a bright summer day.

Do an experiment to see whether coating the plastic wrap with clear sunscreen prevents the paper under the plastic from fading.

Fig. 1. Cut shapes out of paper or card stock.

Fig. 2. Arrange the shapes on a piece of colorful paper

Fig. 3. Find a sunny spot where your project won't be disturbed.

Fig. 4. Cover the paper with plastic wrap to secure the shapes you cut.

Fig. 5. A stencil will also work well for this project.

Fig. 6. After several hours in the sun, check your sun print.

THE STORY BEHIND THE CHEMISTRY

The Sun emits an enormous amount of energy. Some of it travels to Earth as light waves. These waves are different distances apart, like waves moving across a lake. Some light waves are very far apart. For example, red light waves are spaced much further apart than violet ones. Ultraviolet (UV) light waves are even closer together—too close together to be detected by human eyes.

Not only are ultraviolet light waves tightly spaced, but they carry enough energy to permanently destroy some chemical bonds. In construction paper, UV light causes chemical changes to the dye in the paper that changes the way it absorbs light. This alters the color of the paper. When colorful paper is partially covered and put in sunlight, UV light destroys chemicals in the exposed paper and bleaches it. The covered-up parts of the paper are protected and don't change color. Molecules in skin can be damaged by UV light as well, which is why wearing sunscreen is a good idea on a sunny day.

LAB 19

Rosalind Franklin b. 1920

DNA STRUCTURE

HIGH SCORER

Born in London, England, in 1920, Rosalind Franklin was the second of five children. A bright child who loved math and reportedly solved equations for fun, Rosalind was athletic as well. She played cricket and field hockey in school, although her music instructor, the composer Gustav Holst, wrote to her parents that she was not skilled in that particular area of study.

ROCKS FULL OF HOLES

In college, Rosalind studied chemistry, as well as French and German. She became friends with a former student of the famous scientist Marie Curie. After graduating, she studied the porous properties of coal, which was important in the development of charcoal filters for gas masks used during World War II. She received her Ph.D. from Cambridge for this work.

X-RAY VISION

When the war was over, Dr. Franklin went work in a French lab that studied different compounds using X-ray diffraction, a technique that bounces energetic X-rays off of objects to make images. She focused her X-rays on coal and then on graphite. Soon she was an expert in a technique called X-ray crystallography, which aims X-rays at crystals to form an image on film, making it possible to determine the structure of molecules.

A TWISTED LADDER

In 1950 Dr. Franklin was working as the X-ray diffraction expert at a lab at Kings College in England, where she was attempting to take a picture of DNA to help scientists understand its structure. DNA is also called the blueprint of life, because it is like a map for living things to reproduce themselves. Franklin's background in chemistry came in handy for expertly preparing DNA samples, and she captured what is now called "Photo 51": the first clear image of DNA. The clear "X" shape of the image, paired with her measurements, revealed that DNA has a spiral geometry and hinted at the distance between atoms. Soon after being shown Dr. Franklin's photograph, without her permission, scientists James Watson and Francis Crick were able to put together their famous double-helix model of DNA.

GONE BUT NOT FORGOTTEN

In her lifetime, Rosalind Franklin was given little, if any credit for her essential contribution to solving DNA's structure. Watson's descriptions of Dr. Franklin in his memoir *The Double Helix* were sexist and dismissive. She died young of cancer, and just four years after her death, Watson, Crick, and Wilkins were awarded the Nobel Prize for their work on DNA. Fortunately today most scientists understand the essential role Franklin played in solving DNA's structure. She also made important contributions to the study of another chemical called RNA and helped decipher the structure of viruses.

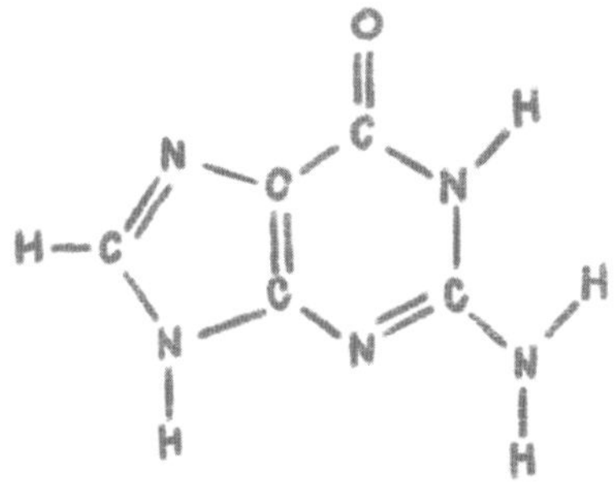

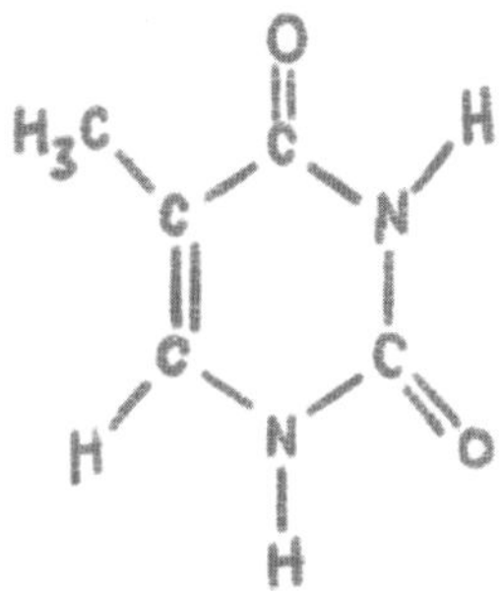

DNA STRUCTURE

Rosalind Franklin prepared DNA samples and took images of them using X-rays. As a result of her work, scientists were able to figure out the chemical and physical structure of DNA. In this lab, you'll create a model of a DNA strand and photograph it from different angles.

Fig. 4. Twist the DNA strand into a double helix.

MATERIALS

- 2 chenille sticks (pipe cleaners)
- Markers in four different colors
- 20 cotton swabs
- Photography device, such as a smart phone or camera

SAFETY TIPS AND HINTS

Spacing the swabs evenly will result a more uniform double helix when you twist the model of the DNA strand.

PROTOCOL

1 Choose 2 chenille sticks (pipe cleaners) that are the same color to form the sugar-phosphate backbone of your DNA strand.

2 Pick a marker color to represent each of the four nucleotides: G, A, T, and C. You should have four colors total. ***Fig. 1.***

3 Once you've assigned a color to a nucleotide, start coloring cotton swabs, half one color and half another color. Each swab will represent a base pair of nucleotides. In DNA, G and C always pair and A and T are always together. Color half of the swabs with the colors you chose for G and C and the other half with the colors you picked for A and T. ***Fig. 2.***

4 Create your own sequence of base pairs by laying out the cotton swabs parallel to one another, varying the colors in an irregular sequence.

5 Tightly wind the chenille sticks around the cotton swabs to create a ladder of base pairs. The swabs should be spaced about 1 inch (2.5 cm) apart. ***Fig. 3.***

6 When you've added as many base pairs to the strand as will fit, twist the DNA strand to create a helical shape. Take a photograph of the DNA strand you constructed. ***Fig. 4.***

7 Observe the double helix from one end, as if looking down a barrel at it. Put it in a cardboard or paper tube, if you wish. To create your own photos take a photograph to replicate the angle of Rosalind Franklin's famous photograph. ***Fig. 5.***

Fig. 1. Choose four colors to represent nucleotides.

Fig. 2. Color cotton swabs to represent base pairs.

Fig. 3. Wind chenille sticks around cotton swabs

Fig. 5. Observe the double helix from the angle it was photographed by Rosalind Franklin.

CREATIVE ENRICHMENT

Place the DNA strand you created on a piece of construction paper or sun print paper in direct sunlight to create a sun print using ultraviolet light. (Lab 18)

THE STORY BEHIND THE CHEMISTRY

DNA, or deoxyribonucleic acid, is a chemical blueprint for life as we know it. Using a basic code, this amazing molecule allows organisms from simple bacteria to incredibly complex humans to grow, thrive, and pass certain traits along to their offspring. The code consists of the letters G, A, T, C, which are organized into long chemical messages that can be translated into building blocks called proteins.

A TWISTED LADDER

The chemical bases that make up DNA are called nucleotides, and there are four of them. Each nucleotide consists of a nitrogen base, a phosphate group, and a sugar. The nitrogen bases are guanine (G), adenine (A), thymine (T) and cytosine (C.) It's easy to picture DNA's double helix as a twisted ladder, with base pairs forming rungs, which are attached to the sides, which scientists call a phosphate backbone. The bases G and C are always paired together, as are A and T.

CODE BREAKER

DNA's double-stranded set of instructions can be unzipped so that certain sequences of code called genes are available to be copied into individual ribbons of RNA (ribonucleic acid.) Messenger RNA moves through translation machines called ribosomes (see Lab 22), which assemble molecules called proteins. Each protein is built from a specific messenger RNA sequence. Besides coding for proteins, DNA and RNA are involved in the processes that regulate what kinds of protein are made, when they are made, and how much of each protein is produced.

LAB 20

Edith Flanigen b. 1929

MOLECULAR SIEVES

A MARVELOUS MENTOR

Edith Flanigen, who was born in 1929 in Buffalo, New York, credits her love of chemistry to a high school teacher. Edith recalls, "She really made (science) exciting. We did hands-on laboratory work, and I think I fell in love with chemistry at that time." Inspired by their teacher, Edith and her two sisters graduated from high school and went on to study chemistry at a nearby college. Following graduation Edith and her sister, Joan, went on to get master's degrees in chemistry from Syracuse University.

CHEMICAL SPONGES AND EMERALDS

The early 1950s found Flanigen and her sisters working at Union Carbide Corporation, despite the fact that there were very few women working in chemistry at the time. Flanigen focused her research on identifying and purifying silicone polymers, which are compounds made up of repeating patterns of similar chemical units. Eventually she moved into a lab that studied molecular sieves, which are like chemical sponges that can mop up small particles while keeping large ones out. Besides working on molecular sieves, Flanigan co-invented synthetic emeralds that were manufactured by Union Carbide and used in pre-laser technology and in jewelry for a few years. She loved the creative, collaborative environment in industry, and helped to foster those ideals in the labs where she worked.

ZEOLITE

In 1973 Flanigen became the first woman named Corporate Research Fellow at Union Carbide, and eventually reached the highest possible technical positions that could be achieved at the corporations where she worked. During her career, she invented and co-invented more than 200 synthetic materials and her name appears on more than 100 patents, which protect new inventions from being copied and sold by someone other than the inventor. Flannigan's research on molecular sieves was especially important. Filtering molecules (groups of atoms) by size allows scientists and industries to separate chemicals compounds. Edith's work with sieve materials called zeolites made it possible to refine oil into its usable parts more safely and efficiently.

PRESIDENTIAL RECOGNITION

In 1983, Flanigen received a Ph.D. from D'Youville College. Besides being inducted into the National Inventors Hall of Fame in 2004, Dr. Edith Flanigan has received countless awards for her work. In 1992 she became the first woman ever awarded the Perkin Medal, and in 2014 President Barack Obama presented her with the National Medal of Technology and Innovation. She is the foremost authority on zeolite chemistry, and her work was the basis of the molecular sieve industry, which produces chemicals we use every day including laundry detergent and cat litter.

GOOD ADVICE

"You have to love (what you do), because if there is any other reason for going into it, it won't work. Secondly, you have to be yourself. You have to recognize your unique characteristics and what your talents are." —Dr. Edith Flanigen

MOLECULAR SIEVES

Experiment with inexpensive natural zeolites to see the variation in them as some trap food coloring and others don't.

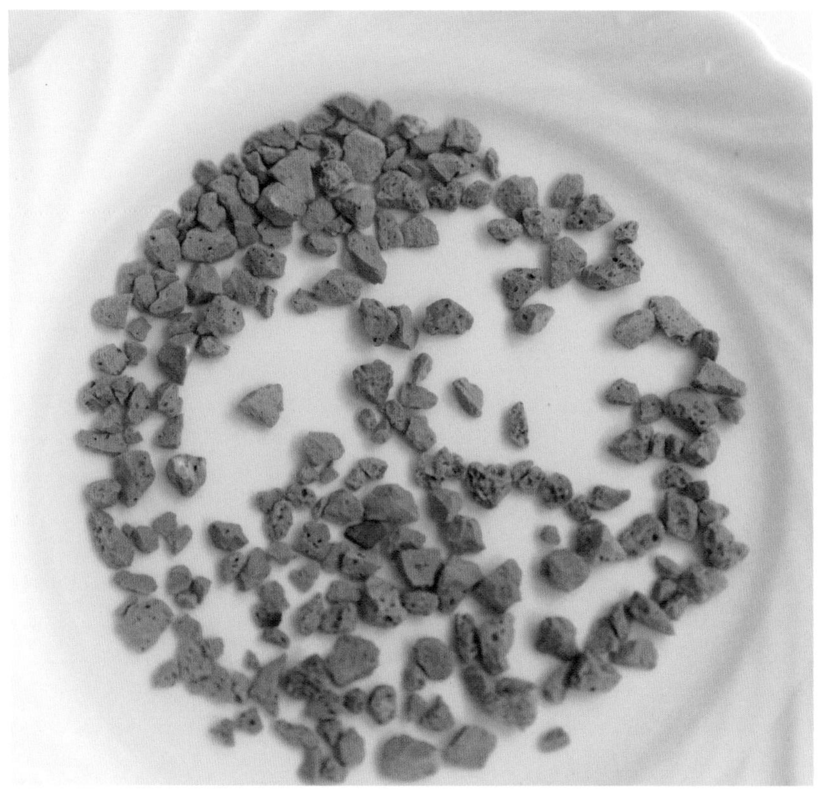

Fig. 5. Rinse and soak zeolites to remove food coloring.

MATERIALS

- Small containers and plates
- Magnifying glass
- Inexpensive natural clinoptilolite zeolite pebbles used for removing ammonia from aquariums (see Resources, page 121)
- Liquid food coloring
- Baking sheet
- Water
- Paper towels
- Thermometer (optional)

SAFETY TIPS AND HINTS

This is a good activity to do outdoors. The clinoptilolite is dusty, and rinse water can be more easily dumped out.

PROTOCOL

1 Put zeolites into four small containers. Study them through a magnifying glass.

2 Drip several drops of food coloring onto them so that each dish contains one color. *Fig. 1.*

3 Mix food coloring and zeolites together. *Fig. 2.*

4 Rinse the zeolites several times with water. Let them sit in water between rinses to allow food coloring time to escape. *Fig. 3.*

5 When most of the stones have returned to their original color, look for zeolite pebbles that have trapped food coloring. *Fig. 4.*

6 Spread the zeolites out on a plate. Observe them under a magnifying glass. Let them dry and observe them again. *Fig. 5.*

7 Bring a glass of water to room temperature. Fill a separate small container such as a jar with zeolites. Make sure the temperature of the zeolites and water is the same.

8 Put the thermometer in the zeolites and record the temperature. Add the room-temperature water to the zeolites until they are just covered and see what happens to the temperature. *Fig. 6.*

CREATIVE ENRICHMENT

Do some research, and design another experiment using zeolites. What other molecules could you trap?

Fig. 1. Drop food coloring onto zeolites.

Fig. 2. Mix in the food coloring.

Fig. 3. Rinse and soak zeolites to remove food coloring.

Fig. 4. Look for zeolites that have trapped food coloring.

Fig. 6. Test the temperature change when room-temperature water is added to zeolites.

THE STORY BEHIND THE CHEMISTRY

Zeolites are three-dimensional crystalline cages made up of the elements aluminum (Al), silicon (Si), and oxygen (O). Natural zeolites such as clinoptilolite have water and other Alkaline Earth Metals (column 2 on the periodic table) trapped between the crystals. These amazing repeated structures contain regular patterns of holes called pores, which are large enough to let very small molecules move through them, but small enough to trap larger molecules. This filtering property gave zeolites the nickname "molecular sieves."

Imagine zeolites as piles of chain-link fences randomly stacked together. If you throw ping-pong balls, tennis balls, and soccer balls at the fences from all sides, some of the ping-pong balls will move all the way through the fences, and the rest can be shaken out. Tennis balls that make their way into the grid will be stuck inside, and soccer balls can't even get into the grid. The holes in the chain link are like the pores in zeolites, and scientists like Edith Flanigan synthesized new kinds of zeolites to trap certain kinds of molecules and keep others out.

Natural zeolites like clinoptilolite contain pores of many different sizes. Clinoptilolite is good at trapping ammonia and is used to remove it from the water in aquariums. This experiment visualizes individual zeolites which contain pores the right size to trap food coloring molecules.

The word zeolite means "boiling stone." Zeolites have an exceptional ability to trap water and hold it inside. As they take water up, zeolites release energy as heat, which you can test in the second part of this lab. When zeolites full of water are heated up (boiled), they will give off steam.

CH_3
H
H_3C
O
O
O
O
H
H
O
CH_3
O

LAB 21

Tu Youyou b. 1930

MEDICINAL PLANT COMPOUNDS

AN INTERRUPTED EDUCATION

Tu Youyou was born in a city on the east coast of China into a family that put a high value on education. The only girl in her family, she attended the best schools in the region until she became sick with tuberculosis when she was sixteen. By the time she had recovered and returned to school two years later, Tu had decided to study medicine so that she could stay healthy and help others. After graduating from high school, she was accepted into the school of pharmacy at the Medical School of Peking University.

PLANTS AS MEDICINE

In her pharmacy courses, Tu learned to study traditional Chinese remedies through the lens of Western medicine. Her professors taught her to identify and classify plants based on their botanical descriptions along with methods for extracting chemical compounds from them. Tu also learned how to characterize the structures of the chemicals she'd isolated. This education helped her to understand how some traditional plants are able to cure disease and her first research project involved studying the effect of an herb called *Lobelia chinensus* on a disease caused by a parasitic flatworm.

A BROKEN FAMILY

During China's Cultural Revolution, many laboratories were shut down and Dr. Youyou was pressured to leave her two young daughters in the care of relatives so she could travel to a laboratory to search for a cure for malaria. Malaria is a deadly disease caused by a parasite spread by mosquitos, and the parasite had become resistant to a number of available medicines. Youyou searched through ancient Chinese texts and folk recipes, searching for new compounds to test against the malaria parasite. She collected more than 2,000 prescriptions to test and went to work experimenting with them.

A CURE

After a number of failures, an herb in the *Artemisia* family show promising results, but she couldn't repeat them consistently. Going back through the old books, she found a recipe that contained a cure for malaria fever that called for "A handful of Qinghao immersed in two liters of water, wring out the juice and drink it all." Dr. Youyou realized that most of the recipes had called for boiling the plant, which may have destroyed the chemical capable of killing the malaria parasite. She followed the heat-free recipe and it killed malaria parasites, so she isolated the fraction containing the active chemical. Due to limited resources, she and two of her colleagues tested the toxicity of the compound by drinking it themselves and found it to be safe enough for clinical trials.

A PRIZE

In 2015 Tu Youyou won the Nobel Prize in Physiology or Medicine for her discovery of artemisinin, a new therapy for malaria. Her discovery has saved millions of lives and is still used today all around the world.

MEDICINAL PLANT COMPOUNDS

In 1972 Tu Youyou reported that she had created an effective treatment for malaria made from a chemical compound she had extracted from the leaves of a plant nicknamed worm-wood, which was a traditional Chinese malaria remedy. In this lab, you'll extract the gel from the leaves of an aloe vera plant to collect a traditional home remedy for sunburn.

Fig. 4. Observe the difference between the inside and outside of each leaf.

MATERIALS

- Aloe vera plant
- Scissors
- Potato peeler
- Knife
- Spoon
- Jar with a lid

SAFETY TIPS AND HINTS

Adult supervision recommended when using sharp knives. A potato peeler works well for this project.

PROTOCOL

1 Cut some leaves off an aloe plant, close to the base of the leaves. Squeeze out the small amount of yellow goo near the cut and discard it. *Fig. 1.*

2 Use a peeler or knife to remove the peel from the underside of an aloe leaf to expose the gel inside. *Fig. 2.*

3 Use a spoon to remove the gel. *Fig. 3.*

4 Observe how the interior of each leaf is dramatically different from the exterior. *Fig. 4.*

5 Put the aloe gel into a jar or another container with a lid. *Fig. 5.*

6 Refrigerate the gel and use it to treat sunburn. *Fig. 6.*

7 Share the fresh aloe gel you collected with your friends and family. *Fig. 7.*

CREATIVE ENRICHMENT

Extract essential oils that can be used as aromatherapy from other plants, including lavender and oranges. (Lab 1)

Fig. 1. Cut a few leaves off of an aloe vera plant and squeeze out the yellow goo near the cut you made.

Fig. 2. Peel off the bottom of an aloe leaf to expose the gel inside.

Fig. 3. Use a spoon to remove the gel.

Fig. 5. Put the aloe gel in a container with a lid.

Fig. 6. Store the aloe vera gel in the refrigerator and use it to sooth irritated skin, sunburn, and other minor skin burns.

Fig. 7. Share the fresh aloe gel with your friends and family.

THE STORY BEHIND THE CHEMISTRY

Many medicines that we still use today were first extracted from plants and used as therapeutic agents for hundreds or thousands of years before being produced in bulk by the pharmaceutical industry. Salicylic acid from willow trees and related plants served as a pain remedy for thousands of years until Bayer started producing a commercial version in 1899. Quinine, an ancient medicine for treating malaria, comes from the bark of the cinchona trees indigenous to Peru, Bolivia, and Ecuador.

However, due to overuse, the malaria parasite developed a resistance to the active components of quinine. Nearly half the world's population lives in areas at risk from malaria. It is extremely fortunate that Dr. Youyou has developed artemisinin therapy, which kills even quinine-resistant malaria parasites.

In this lab, you'll extract aloe gel from leaves. Aloe vera has been used as a skin balm since the time of the ancient Egyptians. It is easy to scrape from the leaves of the succulent plant and feels soothing on sunburns. There is little scientific evidence that aloe vera gel has healing properties, but extracting it is an interesting way to get a look into the world of plant pharmaceuticals.

LAB 22

Ada Yonath b. 1939

RIBOSOME STRUCTURE

FALLING FOR SCIENCE

Ada Yonath set the stage for her scientific career early on. During an ill-conceived childhood experiment, she broke her arm falling from a stack of furniture she was using to measure the height of a balcony. Ada also recalls being inspired at a young age by a biography of Marie Curie.

A STRUGGLE

Ada Yonath's parents were from Poland, but they had left their home country to move to Jerusalem, where they struggled with poverty. Her father suffered from life-threatening health problems, but he and her mother had big dreams for Ada and did everything possible to ensure that she got a good education. After he died when she was only eleven, Ada and her mother worked for a year trying to make ends meet before moving to Tel Aviv around 1951 to be closer to relatives who could help them.

INTRODUCTION TO CRYSTALLOGRAPHY

In college Ada studied chemistry, biochemistry, and biophysics before going on to work toward her Ph.D. at the Weismann Institute of Science. For her doctorate research, she studied the structure of a protein called collagen using X-ray crystallography, which bombards crystals with X-rays to determine their structure. After being awarded her Ph.D., she did postdoctorate research in the United States before returning home as Dr. Ada Yonath to establish the first biological crystallography laboratory in Israel.

MOUNT EVEREST

In the late 1970s, Dr. Yonath decided to tackle a monumental project. She wanted to discover the three-dimensional structure of ribosomes, which are the cellular machines that translate genetic material called RNA into proteins. Ribosomes are complex structures made up of two parts called subunits, and although many scientists told her that what she'd proposed couldn't be done, Ada was determined. Later, she compared her research journey to "climbing Mt. Everest only to discover that a higher Everest stood in front of us."

POLAR BEARS AND RIBOSOMES

To study the structure of ribosomes, first Dr. Yonath had to discover how to crystallize them. After reading about how the ribosomes in polar bears become neatly stacked during hibernation, Dr. Yonath got the idea to isolate organized ribosomes from bacteria that live in extremely cold, hot, or radioactive environments. She figured out how to flash freeze these crystallized ribosome structures and bombard them with X-rays. The results of her work allowed Ada to begin putting together the puzzle of ribosomal structure. By 2001, her lab published the first complete three-dimensional structures of both subunits of the bacterial ribosome. In 2001 Ada Yonath was awarded the Nobel Prize for discovering the structure and function of the ribosome, and her work has proved essential for the production of new antibiotics.

RIBOSOME STRUCTURE

Make a ribosomal model using a stick to represent a messenger RNA strand, bell peppers to represent ribosomes, and candy to act as amino acids.

Fig. 6. Get several "ribosomes" moving along the RNA strand at once.

MATERIALS

- Long stick, dowel, or yard stick (meter stick)
- 1–4 pieces of string, twine, or thin rope (cut a little longer than the stick)
- Candy with a hole in the center, such as Life Savers
- 1–4 large bell peppers, one for each piece of string
- Tape
- Markers

SAFETY TIPS AND HINTS

String all of the peppers onto the dowel and ropes before you start adding candy.

PROTOCOL

1 Write a random series of Gs, As, Ts, Cs on a long dowel or meter stick to represent a strand of RNA (ribonucleic acid.) ***Fig. 1.***

2 Tie a piece of string or rope to one end of the stick for each bell pepper that you will use. Tape the knot(s) to the stick. ***Fig. 2.***

3 Each bell pepper will represent a ribosome. Cut a hole in each end (stem and bottom) of a bell pepper. Cut a third hole in the side of the pepper. Thread the pepper lengthwise onto the dowel or meter stick, and pull the string through the third hole on the pepper. ***Fig. 3.***

4 Tape the end of string or rope to make it easy to thread candy onto it.

5 Pull the pepper and free end of the string to the end of the to the end of the dowel or meter stick farthest from the knot. Slowly move the pepper along the stick to represent how a ribosome moves along an RNA strand.

6 Thread candy on the string coming out of the pepper as it moves to represent an elongating amino acid chain. ***Fig. 4.***

7 The amino acid chain will grow longer and longer as you move the bell pepper ribosome down the stick representing an RNA strand. ***Fig. 5.***

8 Get several ribosomes moving at once. When you're done, cut your "protein" strand off and make a candy necklace. ***Fig. 6.***

CREATIVE ENRICHMENT

Make a model of DNA, deoxyribonucleic acid, which is the template for RNA. (Lab 19)

Fig. 1. Write a series of random G, A, T, Cs on a long dowel or meter stick.

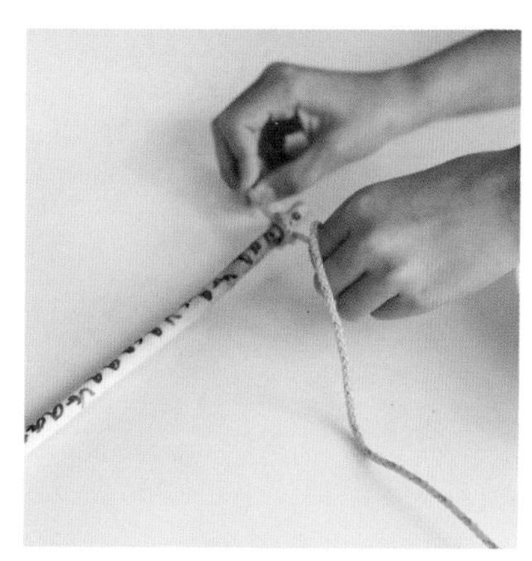

Fig. 2. Tie rope or string to one end of the dowel or meter stick.

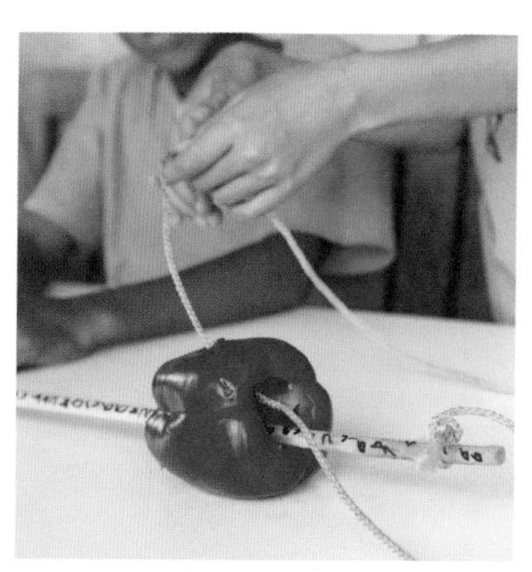

Fig. 3. Cut holes in each end of the pepper and one on top. Thread pepper on ruler and string through the top hole.

Fig. 4. Pull the pepper down the stick, threading candy on the string as it gets longer.

Fig. 5. The candy chain representing amino acids will grow as the pepper "ribosome" moves along the RNA strand stick.

THE STORY BEHIND THE CHEMISTRY

Living things are made up of four types of chemical building blocks: nucleic acids, proteins, carbohydrates, and lipids (fats). Nucleic acids like DNA (deoxyribonucleic acid) and RNA (ribonucleic acid) contain the information required to make proteins. During a process called transcription, messages in DNA are replicated by RNA strands. These messenger RNAs then travel to ribosomes to be translated into proteins.

The nucleic acids that make up DNA are G (guanine), A (adenine), T (thymine), and C (cytosine). RNA is composed of G, A, and C, but instead of T (thymine), it contains U (uracil). Messenger RNA strands are long strings of three-letter codes called codons. Depending on the code, each RNA codon can pair up with a specific chemical called an amino acid. The human body has twenty different amino acids that regularly pair with RNA codons.

Ribosomes are protein-making stations within the cells of living thing. As messenger RNA moves through a ribosome, special RNA called transfer RNA (tRNA) carries amino acids to their matching codons to create long strings of amino acids that are chemically stitched together and then folded to create active protein molecules.

LAB 23

Margaret Cairns Etter b. 1943

CRYSTALLOGRAPHY

SCIENCE WITH A SMILE

Born in 1943 and nicknamed "Peggy," Margaret Carins Etter loved people and science and especially liked people who do science. Her students, friends, and co-workers recall her laugh echoing down hallways and the smiley-face stickers she jokingly gave colleagues when they got good results in the lab. Etter was famous for always doing what she considered to be the right thing, even if it meant risking her career, and she made enormous contributions to science in a relatively short amount of time.

10,000 LAKES

Peggy Etter was born in Delaware, and her father was a chemist at DuPont Experimental Station. She grew up surrounded by scientists who worked with her dad and she went to the University of Pennsylvania to study chemistry. After earning a master's degree at the University of Delaware, Peggy moved to Minnesota, the Land of 10,000 Lakes, where she earned a Ph.D. and settled down to teach for a year at Augustana College before going to work at 3M.

THE BIG PICTURE

Eventually, Dr. Etter returned to the University of Minnesota where she became a full professor and dove into more research. She made important discoveries by studying patterns of hydrogen bonding patterns in chemical structures, rather than focusing on individual bonds. Etter was also fascinated by crystal growth and was one of the first scientists to observe and investigate the strange phenomenon of "jumping crystals" which are now studied in a field of chemistry called mechanochemistry.

AN ADVOCATE

As she explored the mysteries of the unknown on her laboratory bench, Etter fought against oppressive traditions in the worlds of industry and academia. According her colleagues, Etter believed that actions spoke louder than words and wasn't afraid to push the boundaries. She spoke at schools to encourage girls to get into science, helped to establish the 3M Visiting Women's Scientist program, and was a director and instructor in their STEP program, which encourages minority students to become scientists.

A LASTING IMPRESSION

Although Dr. Etter died when she was only forty-nine, she left the chemistry world a better place. Her former students, colleagues, and close friends wrote a number of tributes to her, recalling her "intelligence, elegant presentation, enthusiasm, and radiant personality" and the fact that "she demonstrated what it meant to show respect and compassion for everyone, irrespective of status or behavior." Besides publishing more than eighty important papers, Peggy Etter was a role model, mentor, and teacher and friend to many scientists. Each year, the University of Minnesota holds an annual Etter Memorial Lecture and the American Crystallographic Association gives two awards in honor of Dr. Etter.

CRYSTALLOGRAPHY

Grow three types of crystals. Compare their growth rate and shapes.

MATERIALS

- 3 raw eggs
- Plates
- Liquid food coloring
- Glue
- ¾ cup (around three 53 g jars) alum (potassium aluminum sulfate)
- 3 cups (672 g) Epsom salt
- 10–12 tablespoons (around ½ cup or 78 g) Borax
- Water
- Magnifying glass
- Heatproof containers
- Chenille sticks or pipe cleaners (optional)

Fig. 6. Remove the crystal-encrusted shells from the solution.

SAFETY TIPS AND HINTS

Adult supervision is required when boiling liquids and cutting eggshells with a serrated knife. Wash your hands after handling raw eggs.

PROTOCOL

1 Gently crack each raw egg along its horizontal axis (long side) and use a serrated knife to cut the shells in half lengthwise.

2 Paint food coloring on the inside of the eggshells and allow it to dry. ***Fig. 1.***

3 Label three plates as alum, Epsom, or Borax. Put 2 eggshells on each plate. Brush glue on the inside of the shells and sprinkle a few crystals on the glue according to the label on the plate. Allow to dry. ***Fig. 2.***

4 In separate heatproof containers, dissolve: the alum in 2 cups (475 ml) of water, the Borax in 3 cups (705 ml) of water, and the Epsom salts in 2 cups (475 ml) of water to make super-saturated solutions. It works well to boil the water, add the crystals, and stir. If the crystals don't completely dissolve, microwave them for 30 seconds, stir, and repeat until they are no longer visible. ***Fig. 3.***

5 Allow the solutions to cool to room temperature.

6 Drop the eggshells into the solution containing the same type of crystals that you sprinkled on the shells. If you have a chenille stick or pipe cleaner, hang it over the edge of the container so that it dangles into the solution. ***Fig. 4.***

7 Let the shells sit in the solution until large crystals form. Some will form quickly, and others will take a day or two to grow. Skim extra crystals off the top of the liquids. ***Fig. 5.***

8 Remove the crystal-encrusted shells from the solution. ***Fig. 6.***

9 Observe the crystals under a magnifying glass. Compare the different crystal shapes. ***Fig. 7.***

Fig. 1. Paint food coloring onto eggshells.

Fig. 2. Brush glue onto eggshells and sprinkle a few crystals onto the glue.

Fig. 3. Dissolve Epsom salts, Borax, and alum in water to make solutions.

Fig. 4. Drop the crystal-seeded eggshells into the matching solutions.

Fig. 5. Let the shells sit in the solutions until larger crystals form.

Fig. 7. Compare the different crystal shapes.

CREATIVE ENRICHMENT

Large sugar crystals can be grown on wooden skewers or craft sticks to make rock candy. Clip off the sharp end of the skewers, dip them in water, and roll them in sugar. Let them dry and then immerse them in sugar syrup made by boiling 5 cups of sugar (800 g) in 2 cups (475 ml) of water until clear and cooling to room temperature.

THE STORY BEHIND THE CHEMISTRY

Crystals are solid materials that grow when atoms or molecules snap together in repeating, organized patterns, like three-dimensional puzzle pieces. Although they may pull in some intruding atoms by accident, they are mostly made up of a single type of molecule, like sodium chloride, which is table salt. Some crystals are made up of a single type of atom, like diamonds, which are carbon crystals formed under pressure.

In this lab, you'll grow three types of transparent (see-through) crystals. Borax, or sodium tetraborate, is a compound used in detergents and as a preservative in contact lens solution. Epsomite, or Epsom salts is used in agriculture and medicine. Alum, which is found in baking powder and used to keep pickles crisp, is also called potassium aluminum sulfate. It is fun to observe that each type of crystal has its own unique shape, whether big or small. Epsomite makes long needles, while alum forms sparkling cubes.

LAB 24

Linda Buck b. 1947

OLFACTORY CHEMISTRY

A HAPPY CHILDHOOD

Linda Buck was born in Seattle in 1947 to parents who encouraged her creativity from the beginning. With a father who was an electrical engineer and a mother who loved puzzles, Buck's childhood primed her for a lifetime of innovative problem-solving. Given the freedom to pursue a number of interests, Linda wasn't sure what she wanted to study in college, but she was drawn to psychology, which is the study of the human mind.

A NONTRADITIONAL PATH

After attending the University of Washington, Linda wasn't sure that she wanted to be a psychotherapist, so she left school to travel but continued taking classes when she could. A course in immunology, which is the science of how our bodies fight infection, got her interested in biology, and she graduated from college with a degree in microbiology and psychology when she was twenty-eight. She moved to Texas to earn a Ph.D. in immunology before going to work in the lab of Richard Axel at Columbia University.

YEARS IN A LAB

In Axel's neuroscience lab, Dr. Buck was fascinated by cells that send signals to the brain and became obsessed with the idea of figuring out which cells in the nose detect scent. She also wanted to understand which genes (DNA codes) are related to these cells, and how the cells can recognize so many different odors. She worked for years to unravel the mystery, trying everything she could think of, with nothing to show for it.

MYSTERY SOLVED

Dr. Buck could hardly believe it when, in 1991, she discovered a group of genes that no one had ever seen before. These genes coded for a group of 350 smell receptors that work in combination to detect thousands of different odors. In 2004 Linda and her colleague Richard Axel shared the Nobel Prize in Physiology or Medicine for their discoveries of odorant receptors and the organization of the olfactory smell system. She said, "As a woman in science, I sincerely hope that my receiving a Nobel Prize will send a message to young women everywhere that the doors are open to them and that they should follow their dreams."

OLFACTORY CHEMISTRY

Use your nose to test your smelling abilities by distinguishing different smells with a blindfold on.

MATERIALS

- Food, flowers, and herbs with a strong smell, such as coffee, chocolate, fresh herbs, and dried flowers
- Plates or dishes
- Blindfold
- Paper and pencil

SAFETY TIPS AND HINTS

Be sure to check whether kids have food allergies before selecting items for this project.

PROTOCOL

1 Collect food items, herbs, and flowers with distinctive, strong smells. *Fig. 1.*

2 For example, mix yeast with warm water. *Fig. 2.*

3 Put the items on individual plates or in dishes. *Fig. 3.*

4 Take turns blindfolding family and friends. Try to identify each item by smell. Write down what each person guesses for different items. *Fig. 4.*

5 Have a contest to see who can identify the most objects by smell. *Fig. 5.*

6 Is it hard to tell certain items apart, like chocolate and coffee, or do they all have distinctive odors? Which items were hardest to identify? *Fig. 6.*

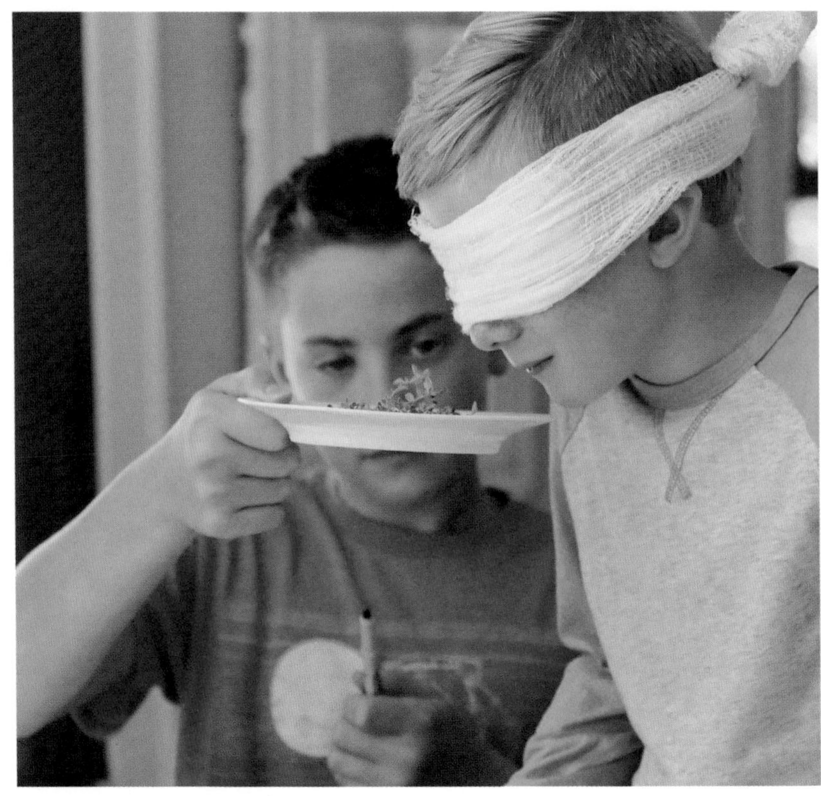

Fig. 6. Which items were hardest to identify?

CREATIVE ENRICHMENT

Choose items that have similar smells and try this experiment again. Can you tell different citrus fruits apart?

Fig. 1. Collect food, flowers, and herbs with distinctive smells.

Fig. 2. For example, mix yeast with warm water and stir.

Fig. 3. Put items on plates.

Fig. 4. Identify the items by smell.

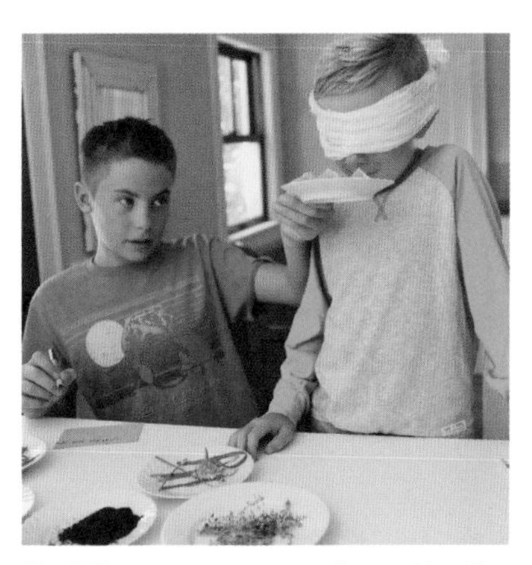

Fig. 5. Have a contest to see who can identify the most smells correctly.

THE STORY BEHIND THE CHEMISTRY

Our sense of smell enhances experiences, such as walking through a flower garden or into a restaurant, but it also alerts us to danger. While most edible foods smell good, most people are repelled by the odor of spoiled and poisonous food. Certain smells can trigger memories, attraction, aggression, and even fear.

Odorants are small, volatile (easily evaporated) molecules that we can smell. These chemicals come in many shapes and sizes, and our noses help us distinguish one smell from another. A very small chemical difference between two molecules can make them smell completely different from one another. For example, two molecules with very similar chemical structures smell very different: one smells like banana and the other one like pear.

Odorants that waft into our noses are immediately detected by nerve cells embedded in a layer of cells called the olfactory epithelium, which lines the nasal cavity. Dr. Buck's work revealed that each of these nerve cells can detect multiple odorants and that individual nerve cells work in concert with their neighbors to decipher what they are detecting.

Olfactory nerves send signals to special organs in our brains, such as the olfactory bulb, and the olfactory cortex. From there, signals travel to other parts of our brain, triggering physical and emotional responses to what we smell. In this lab, you put your olfactory nerves to work by distinguishing familiar odorants from one another.

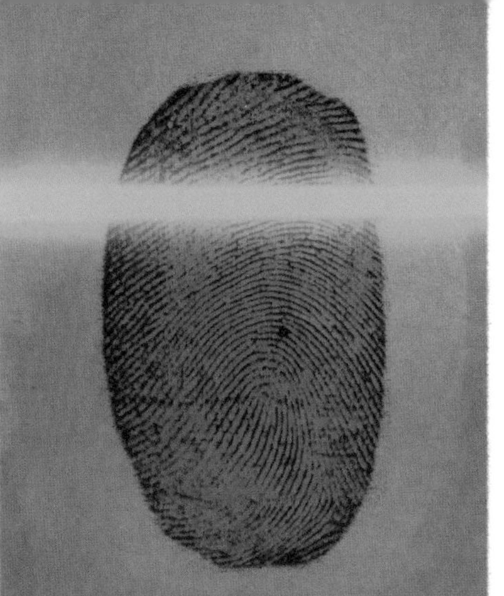
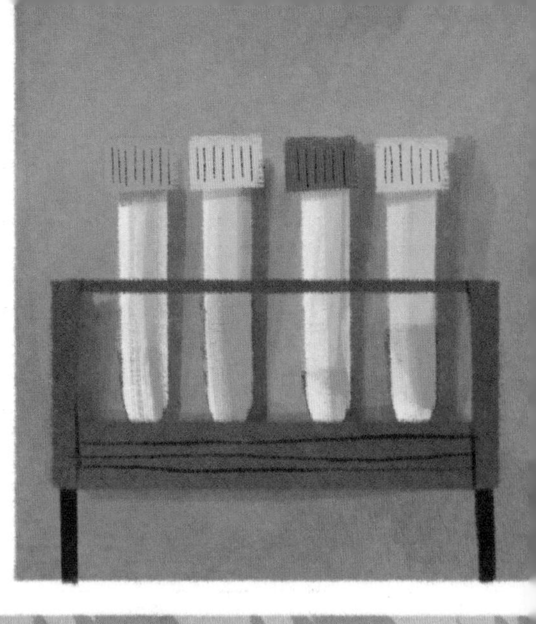

H_3C
CH_3
O_2N
NO_2
NO_2

LAB 25

Raychelle Burks b. 1975

COLORIMETRIC SENSORS

CALIFORNIA KID

Growing up in California, Raychelle Burks loved going to the library and solving mysteries alongside the sleuths of her favorite detective stories. Her family spent hours having long discussions about books and movies, which fueled her curiosity about popular culture. As she grew, their conversations around television shows such as *Star Trek* inspired her to think critically about what she observed in the world around her.

SUPER SLEUTH

Raychelle's grandmother had introduced her to Agatha Christie, and she was drawn to the observant characters who assembled information in an orderly way to piece together a possible scenario. As a teenager, a visit to a forensic science lab showed her how scientific equipment and chemical tests could be used to lead investigators to discoveries about crimes. She realized that science was a vehicle that could turn her passion for solving mysteries into a career.

REAL-LIFE TRICORDER

After pursuing her education, Dr. Burks spent a few years working in a crime lab before returning to academia. Today, she is a professor of chemistry who studies colorimetric sensors for chemical identity and concentration determination. She uses forensic science research to help reveal clues, doubling up as a science communication superhero when she's not busy with molecular sleuthing in her laboratory.

PORTABLE CHEMICAL SENSOR

The chemical sensor Dr. Burks is working to develop in her lab is astonishingly similar to the fictional tricorder on *Star Trek*, which is also a hand-held device used to scan the environment. Her current research efforts are focused on the design of sensing systems that can identify chemical clues tied to crime and uses smartphones, laptops, and tablets as scientific analytical devices.

SCI-COMM SUPERHERO

As a science communicator and role model for aspiring scientists, Burks uses popular culture as a positive space for discussions about society, science, and stereotypes. In the classroom, online, and beyond, she works to ignite appreciation of chemistry through hands-on projects and pop culture references. Burks helped create and organize *SciPop Talks!*, a popular talk series blending science and pop culture. She appears regularly on television, podcasts, and at genre conventions, and she owns a cheweenie, which is a cross between a dachshund and a chihuahua.

AWARDS

Dr. Burks was awarded the 2019 Mindlin Foundation Science Communication Prize and the 2020 American Chemical Society James T. Grady-James H. Stack Award for Interpreting Chemistry for the Public. In 2019 she was selected as an AAAS If/Then Ambassador by the American Association for the Advancement of Science and the Lyda Hill Philanthropies.

SMART SENSING

Use your smartphone as a spectrometer using a clear cup, a box, and a colorimeter app.

MATERIALS

- Water
- Measuring cup and spoons
- 6 small clear cups
- Red sports beverage
- Cardboard box
- Green construction paper
- Red cabbage (optional)
- White vinegar (optional)
- Baking soda (optional)
- Smartphone with a colorimeter app capable of detecting RGB (red, green, and blue)

SAFETY TIPS AND HINTS

- An inexpensive colorimeter app on a smartphone is required to perform this experiment.
- Rather than pouring samples in and out of a sample holder, it's possible to engineer the hole in the box to hold the mixing cups, so that you can simply switch cups to take readings.

PROTOCOL

1 Measure ¼ cup (60 ml) of water into four clear cups. ***Fig. 1.***

2 Add ¼ cup (60 ml) of red sports drink to the fifth cup. This is your undiluted sample. ***Fig. 2.***

3 Make 1 to 4 serial dilutions. Add 4 teaspoons (3 to 4 ml) from the red sports drink cup into the cup of water next to it. Mix and add 4 teaspoons from that cup into the next cup. Mix and repeat with until you have 4 dilutions of the red drink. ***Fig. 3.***

Fig. 7. Record the RGB values of red sports drink and each dilution.

You will have the following samples:

Undiluted

- 1:4
- 1:16
- 1:64
- 1:256

4 Choose a clear vessel such as a small cup, glass, or jar to hold samples. Cut windows in a cardboard box and tape it shut so that light can shine through the front of the box, through the sample, and out through the back of the box. You'll have to cut a hole in the top for the sample container so that it can be easily removed for changing samples. ***Fig. 4.***

5 Put green paper behind the box. Taping it to a wall works well. Place the box in front of the paper, leaving a little space between them for light.

6 Open the colorimeter app on a smartphone. Position the device in front of the box so that the phone can "see" through the box and clear container to the green paper behind the box. ***Fig. 5.***

7 Fill the glass in the box with water and record the baseline R (red), G (green), and Blue (blue) readings for water. ***Fig. 6.***

8 Test and record the RGB readings for undiluted red drink and for each dilution, rinsing the cup with water before adding a new sample. Save the dilutions so you can use them again. ***Fig. 7.***

Fig. 1. Measure water into four clear cups.

Fig. 2. Add red sports drink to a fifth cup.

Fig. 3. Make a series of dilutions.

Fig. 4. Cut and tape a box so that light can shine through a clear vessel and out the back of the box.

Fig. 5. Position the device so that it can "see" through the sample container onto green paper.

Fig. 6. Record the RGB values of water.

9 Do a blind test by having someone choose one of the dilutions. Test the RGB readings and see if you can determine which dilution it is.

Optional: Make some cabbage juice (Lab 15) and add a spoonful of baking soda to a cup of it see how a basic solution makes the solution turn blue. To cabbage juice in a second cup, add vinegar, an acid, to see how it turns the colorful pigment from purple to pink. ***Fig. 8.***

10 Use your colorimetry app to test the RGB readings of purple cabbage juice with a neutral pH. Then test the readings after you've added baking soda or vinegar. ***Fig. 9.***

Fig. 9. Test how the RGB readings can change for an acid-base indicator, depending on whether you add an acid or base.

THE STORY BEHIND THE CHEMISTRY

Scientists are becoming more and more interested in using portable devices such as smartphones in their work. Not only are these devices well-equipped to collected data from the environment, but they can perform complicated data-processing tasks very quickly.

Light waves that human eyes can easily detect are part of what scientists call the visible spectrum. The primary colors red, green, and blue can be combined in various proportions to obtain every color of the rainbow. Colors we see, from orange butterflies to blue sky, contain a certain percentage of red, green, and blue (RGB). By discovering the RGB ratios of a certain hue, it's possible to define and replicate any color, making it easy to match paint colors, for example.

Colorimeters are devices that measure the visible light absorbed by material. In this lab, natural or electric light is reflected off of green paper, passes through liquid in a clear sample cup, and travels to the camera lens on a phone. Using data from light sensors in the phone's camera, a colorimeter app can calculate the percentage of red, green, and blue light reaching the lens.

This lab makes it simple to use a smartphone as a spectrometer, a device that can use light wave absorption to calculate the type and concentration of molecules in a solution. When clear liquid tested, mostly green light waves are reflected off the green paper and back to the phone and the G reading is high. If red liquid is added to the sample holder in this lab, it absorbs some of the light waves being reflected by the green paper, and the G value will drop. This experiment works best when the background paper is the complimentary color of the sample you are testing.

Fig. 8. Make some cabbage juice and test how it reacts to adding an acid or a base.

CREATIVE ENRICHMENT

Make an acid-base indicator from cabbage juice to see how a single chemical can change color in acidic and basic solutions. How could you use a color-changing chemical to detect a clue in a criminal lab?

GLOSSARY

Atom
Smallest particle of matter that has unique chemical properties. Atoms are made of fundamental particles called electrons, protons and neutrons. Most of the atomic mass comes from the protons and neutrons in the nucleus.

Carbonation
The process of combining carbon dioxide with a liquid

Carbon Dioxide
A heavy colorless gas formed by burning fuels, by the breakdown or burning of animal and plant matter, and by the act of breathing

Chemistry
A science that deals with the composition and properties of substances and of the changes they undergo

Condensation
The conversion of a vapor to a liquid (as by cooling)

Distillation
The process of heating a liquid until it evaporates into a gas, and then cooling the gas until it becomes liquid

DNA
Deoxyribonucleic acid: A self-replicating molecule found in the chromosomes of in living organisms which carries a sequence of genetic information

Electron
A fundamental particle of matter with negative electric charge, forming a cloud outside the nucleus of an atom

Evaporation
The process of changing from a liquid to a gas

Gene
A basic unit of heredity found on DNA which allows genetic information to be passed from parent to offspring and codes for the synthesis of RNA, from which proteins are assembled

Hypothesis
A proposed explanation for a phenomenon that requires further study or investigation

Matter
The substance of which a physical object is composed

Molecule
Two or more atoms held together by chemical bonds

Neutron
A fundamental particle of matter with no electric charge which forms part of the nucleus of an atom

Nucleus (atomic)
The dense center region of an atom, which contains protons and neutrons

Oxygen
A chemical element found in that air as a colorless, odorless, tasteless gas that is necessary for life

Pigment
A substance that gives color to other materials

Polymer
A chemical compound made of molecules that are arranged in a simple repeating pattern to form a chain structure

Protein
A large molecule made up of one or more long chains of amino acids

Proton
A fundamental particle of matter with positive electric charge which forms part of the nucleus of the atom

Ribosome
A structure which serves as a factory for protein synthesis in cells

RNA
Ribonucleic acid: A messenger molecule which carries chemical codes for the synthesis of proteins and regulates gene expression

Solution
A solid, liquid, or gas dissolved in a liquid

RESOURCES AND REFERENCES

RESOURCES

The Melt and Pour soap base for Lab 2, can be purchased online and at craft retailer stores

Beverage containers with spigots, steel wool, and washing soda, for Labs 4, 5, and 11, can be purchased online or at general merchandise and hardware stores.

5mm LEDs for Lab 6, can be purchased online and at some electronics stores

You can buy zeolites for Lab 20 from online retailers, such as Amazon or Chewy.com. Look for Marineland White Diamond Ammonia Neutralizing Crystals (50 ounces [1.4 kg])

Please see the following articles to learn more about using a mobile device as an absorption spectrometer.

Kuntzleman, Tom. "Use Your Smartphone as an 'Absorption Spectrophotometer.'" *ChemEd X*, March 30, 2016. www.chemedx.org/blog/use-your-smartphone-absorption-spectrophotometer.

Kuntzleman, Tom., and Erik C. Jacobson. "Teaching Beer's Law and Absorption Spectrophotometry with a Smart Phone: A Substantially Simplified Protocol." *Journal of Chemical Education*, 93, no. 7 (2016): 1249–1252. doi.org/10.1021/acs.jchemed.5b00844. pubs.acs.org/doi/abs/10.1021/acs.jchemed.5b00844#.

McGonigle, Andrew, Thomas Wilkes, Tom Pering, et al. "Smartphone Spectrometers." *Sensors (Basel)*, 18, no. 1 (2018): 223. doi:10.3390/s18010223. www.ncbi.nlm.nih.gov/pmc/articles/PMC5796291.

REFERENCES

Linda Buck

Buck, Linda. Nobel Lecture: Unraveling the Sense of Smell. December 8, 2004. www.nobelprize.org/prizes/medicine/2004/buck/lecture.

"Richard Axel and Linda Buck Awarded 2004 Nobel Prize in Physiology or Medicine." Howard Hughes Medical Institute. October 4, 2004. www.hhmi.org/news/richard-axel-and-linda-buck-awarded-2004-nobel-prize-physiology-or-medicine.

Raychelle Burks

"Raychelle Burks // Pop Culture Chemist." Josie and The Podcast. player.fm/series/josie-and-the-podcast/raychelle-burks-pop-culture-chemist.

Marie Curie

Curie, Marie Sklodowska. "Radium and Radioactivity." *Century Magazine*. January 1904: 461–466. cwp.library.ucla.edu/Phase2/Curie,_Marie_Sklodowska@812345678.html.

Margaret Etter

Bernstein, Joel. "Peggy Etter: A Personal Recollection." *Crystal Growth & Design*, 16, no. 3 (2016): 1135–1143. doi: 10.1021/acs.cgd.5b01296. pubs.acs.org/doi/10.1021/acs.cgd.5b01296.

Edith Marie Flanigen

Moriarty, Barbara. "Dr. Edith Marie Flanigen." Women Chemists Committee. March 30, 2005. web.archive.org/web/20140106033133/http://chicagoacs.net/WCC/flanigen.html.

Dmitri Mendeleev

Johanson, Christine. *Women's Struggle for Higher Education in Russia, 1855–1900*. McGill-Queen's Press-MQUP, 1987.

Agnes Pockels

Helm, Christiane A. "Agnes Pockels: Life, Letters and Papers." In *APS March Meeting Abstracts*. 2004.

Ada Yonath

"Ada E. Yonath: Biography." Nobel Prize in Chemistry 2009. www.nobelprize.org/prizes/chemistry/2009/yonath/biographical.

THE PERIODIC TABLE

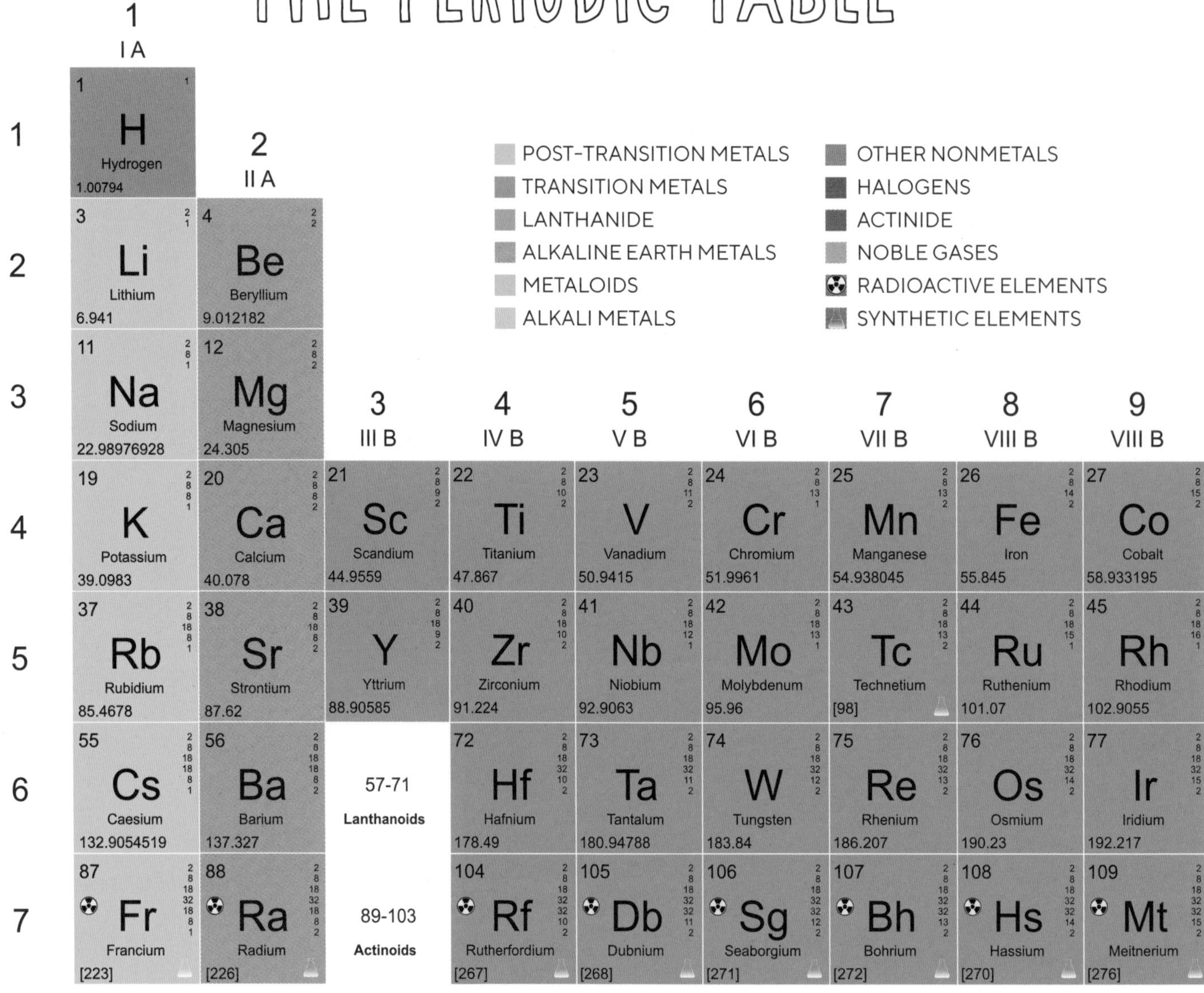

Lanthanoids	57 La Lanthanum 138.90547	58 Ce Cerium 140.116	59 Pr Praseodymium 140.90765	60 Nd Neodymium 144.242	61 Pm Promethium [145]	62 Sm Samarium 150.36	63 Eu Europium 151.964
Actinoids	89 Ac Actinium [227]	90 Th Thorium 232.03806	91 Pa Protactinium 231.03588	92 U Uranium 238.02891	93 Np Neptunium [237]	94 Pu Plutonium [244]	95 Am Americium [243]

Matter is made up of invisible building blocks called atoms. The atoms of any given element are identical, and consist of three basic particles: protons, electrons, and neutrons. A nucleus, found at the center of each atom, contains the positively charged protons and the neutrons, which carry no charge. The outermost regions of the atom, which contain negatively charged electrons, are called electron shells.

Study the Periodic Table above. See how many elements you recognize. Find the atomic number in the upper left-hand corner of each element. This number tells you how many protons the element has in its nucleus. At the bottom of each square, you'll find the element's atomic mass, which is not a whole number, because the number of neutrons might vary. The number you see is an average and you can round it to the nearest whole number. To calculate how many neutrons are in an element, subtract the atomic number from the atomic mass.

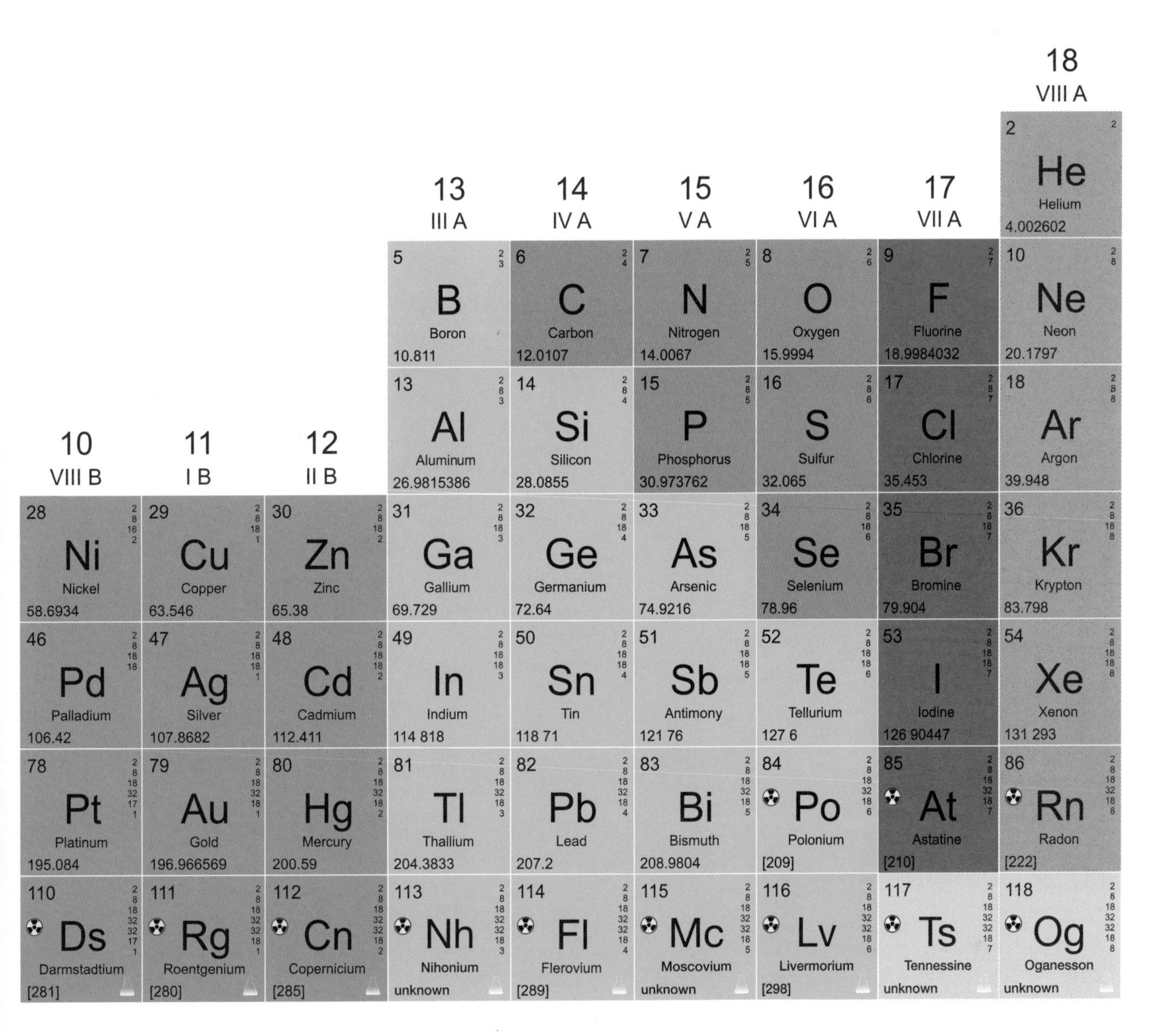

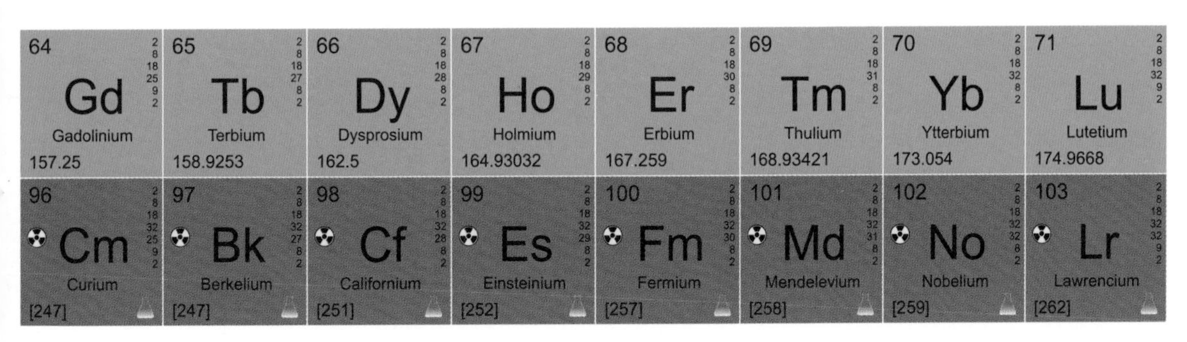

Atoms always have the same number of protons and electrons. Simply look at the atomic number to see how many electrons an element has. On the right side of each square, some periodic tables show you how the electrons are arranged in their shells, with the number on top representing the number of electrons in the shell closest to the nucleus.

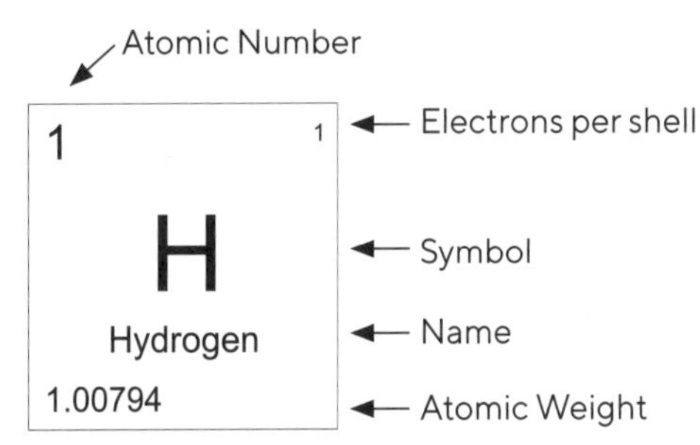

ACKNOWLEDGMENTS

My family, and especially Ken, Sarah, May, and Charlie, who live surrounded by the chaos of my science adventures.

My dad and physics advisor, Ron Lee.

Amber Procaccini, whose photographs capture kids doing science projects so beautifully and transform everyday objects into art.

Kelly Anne Dalton, whose stunning illustrations create brilliant portraits of the scientists featured in this book.

The smart, funny kids whose smiles illuminate these pages, and their parents.

Susan Nackers Ludwig, errand runner and assistant extraordinaire.

Jonathan Simcosky, Mary Ann Hall, Heather Godin, Nyle Vialet, Jenna Nelson, and the rest of the team at Quarry Books who brought this book to life.

Rhea Lyons, my amazing agent.

ABOUT THE AUTHOR

Liz Heinecke has loved science since she was old enough to inspect her first caterpillar. After working in molecular biology research for ten years, she left the lab to kick off a new chapter in her life as a stay-at-home mom. Soon she found herself sharing her love of science with her three kids and journaling their experiments and adventures on KitchenPantryScientist.com.

In addition to running her website, Liz regularly demonstrates science on television and writes books. Her list of publications includes: *Kitchen Science Lab for Kids*, *Outdoor Science Lab for Kids*, *STEAM Lab for Kids*, *Star Wars Maker Lab*, and *Kitchen Science Lab for Kids, Edible Edition*. When she's not writing or doing science outreach, you'll find Liz at home in Minnesota, singing, playing banjo, painting, running, and doing almost anything else to avoid housework.

Liz graduated from Luther College where she studied art and biology. She received her master's degree in bacteriology from the University of Wisconsin, Madison.

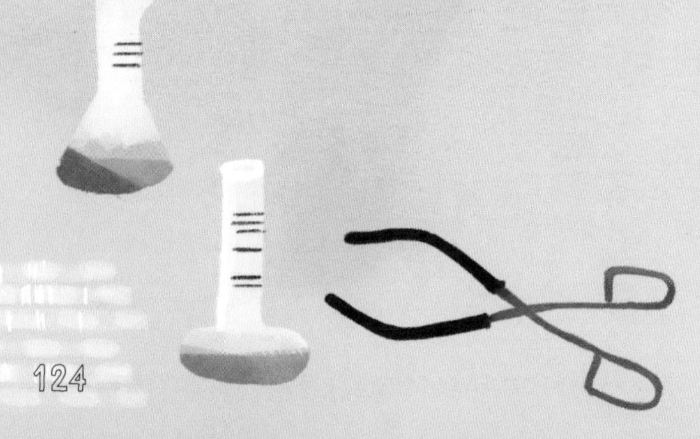

ABOUT THE PHOTOGRAPHER

Amber Procaccini is a commercial and editorial photographer based in Minneapolis, Minnesota. She specializes in photographing kids, babies, food, and travel, and her passion for photography almost equals her passion for finding the perfect taco.

Amber met Liz while photographing her first book, *Kitchen Science Lab for Kids*, and she knew they'd make a great team when they bonded over cornichons, pate, and brie. When Amber isn't photographing eye-rolling tweens or making cheeseburgers look mouthwatering, she and her husband love to travel and enjoy new adventures together.

ABOUT THE ILLUSTRATOR

Kelly Anne Dalton is a professional artist and illustrator living in the Victorian gold rush town of Helena, Montana. Working from her charming 1920s studio, Kelly Anne loves creating a wide range of work, from pattern design to children's books. With a degree in economics, Kelly was happy to combine her love of historical research and science in her illustrations.

When not drawing, Kelly Anne enjoys trail running in the mountains, playing with her dogs, and traveling with her husband.

Index

P

R

S

T

U

V

X

Y